BrightRED Study Guide

Curriculum for Excellence

N5

BUSINESS MANAGEMENT

William Reynolds

First published in 2014 by:
Bright Red Publishing Ltd
1 Torphichen Street
Edinburgh
EH3 8HX

Reprinted with corrections 2016 and 2017
Copyright © Bright Red Publishing Ltd 2014

Cover image © Caleb Rutherford

A CIP record for this book is available from the British Library

ISBN 978-1-906736-33-0

With thanks to:
PDQ Digital Media Solutions Ltd (layout) and Sue Moody, Bright Writing (edit)

Cover design and series book design by Caleb Rutherford – e i d e t i c

Acknowledgements
Every effort has been made to seek all copyright holders. If any have been overlooked, then Bright Red Publishing will be delighted to make the necessary arrangements.

Permission has been sought from all relevant copyright holders and Bright Red Publishing are grateful for the use of the following:
Sergey Nivens/Shutterstock.com (p 6); Monkey Business Images/Shutterstock.com (p 6); zeafonzo/Stock-Xchnge (p 8); rubinsheto/Stock-Xchnge (p 8); Steven Lilley CC BY-SA 2.0)[1] (p 10); Tim Green (CC BY 2.0)[2] (p 10); McGoo84/Stock-Xchnge (p 10); Logo © Domino's Pizza Group Limited. All rights reserved (p 15); Logo © Doctor's Associates Inc. SUBWAY® is a registered trademark of Doctor's Associates Inc (p 15); Logo © Starbucks Corporation (p 15); Logo used with permission from McDonald's Restaurants Limited, information correct as of date of publication (p 19); Logo © KFC (p 21); Logo © Greggs plc (p 21); Logo © Next Group Plc (p 21); Ell Brown (CC BY 2.0)[2] (p 22); 1000 Words/Shutterstock.com (p 25); CannedTuna (CC BY 2.0)[2] (p 25); sergign/Shutterstock.com (p 26); Tomasz Trojanowski/Shutterstock.com (p 28); Racorn/Shutterstock.com (p 28); Andrey_Popov/Shutterstock.com (p 29); Aaron Amat/Shutterstock.com (p 31); Andresr/Shutterstock.com (p 31); Konstantin Chagin/Shutterstock.com (p 32); Lisa F. Young/Shutterstock.com (p 34); ostill/Shutterstock.com (p 34); © mast3r/Shutterstock.com (p 37); Todtanis (CC BY-SA 3.0)[3] (p 38); 'Health and Safety Law: what you need to know' poster © Health and Safety Executive. Contains public sector information licensed under the Open Government Licence v2.0 (p 40); Images_of_Money (CC BY 2.0)[2] (p 42); ota_photos CC BY-SA 2.0)[1] (p 43); 401(K) 2012 CC BY-SA 2.0)[1] (p 47); © Robert Kneschke/Shutterstock.com (p 50); Paul Stocker (CC BY 2.0)[2] (p 53); Jag_cz/Shutterstock.com (p 56); Craig Parylo/Stock-Xchnge (p 58); gokoroko/Stock-Xchnge (p 58); Mariusz Niedzwiedzki/Shutterstock.com (p 59); Clubcard image © Tesco PLC (p 61); Irn-Bru image © A.G. Barr (p 63); Tipp-Ex image © BIC UK & IRELAND LTD (p 63); Sellotape logo © Henkel Ltd (p 63); MARS is a registered trademark of Mars, Incorporated. The trademark is used with permission. Mars, Incorporated is not associated with Bright Red Publishing Ltd. The image of the MARS bar is printed with permission of Mars, Incorporated. (p 65); Persil image © Unilever Plc (p 65); Tesco Everyday Value Baked Beans image © Tesco PLC (p 66); Asda Smart Price Baked Beans © Asda Stores Ltd (p 66); Fairy Liquid image © Procter & Gamble (p 67); Kellogg's Cornflakes image © Kellogg Co (p 67); Innocent Orange Juice image © innocent ltd (p 67); Nescafe Coffee image © Nestlé Group (p 67); Ranglen/Shutterstock.com (p 69); ilco/Stock-Xchnge (p 72); kalilo/Stock-Xchnge (p 72); iprole/Stock-Xchnge (p 72); Konstantins Visnevskis/Shutterstock.com (p 72); Dan Kosmayer/Shutterstock.com (p 72); CWA Studios/Shutterstock.com (p 74); Pearson Scott Foresman (public domain) (p 77); Adil 649 (CC BY-SA 3.0)[3] (p 77); Vik Olliver (GFDL v1.2)[5] (p 77); Pavel L Photo and Video/Shutterstock.com (p 78); Desert Botanical Garden (CC BY-ND 2.0)[4] (p 78); Recycling symbol (public domain) (p 83); Text from the Thomson Holidays website © TUI UK Limited (p 88); Text from the ASDA website © Asda Stores Ltd (p 89).

(CC BY-SA 2.0)[1] http://creativecommons.org/licenses/by-sa/2.0/
(CC BY 2.0)[2] http://creativecommons.org/licenses/by/2.0/
(CC BY-SA 3.0)[3] http://creativecommons.org/licenses/by-sa/3.0/
(CC BY-ND 2.0)[4] http://creativecommons.org/licenses/by-nd/2.0/
(GFDL v1.2)[5] http://www.gnu.org/licenses/fdl-1.2.html#SEC1

Printed and bound in the UK.

CONTENTS LIST

BRIGHTRED STUDY GUIDE: NATIONAL 5 BUSINESS MANAGEMENT

UNDERSTANDING BUSINESS

MANAGEMENT OF PEOPLE AND FINANCE

MANAGEMENT OF MARKETING AND OPERATIONS

CASE STUDIES

GLOSSARY

INTRODUCTION

Business organisations play an important role in society. Every day we come into contact with organisations ranging from supermarkets, restaurants, hotels and retail outlets to leisure centres, hospitals and libraries. We all rely on businesses to organise the economic resources that create the goods and services which satisfy consumers' needs and wants. The economy also depends on organisations to create employment opportunities, income and wealth for members of the workforce. It is, therefore, essential that society develops competent and innovative entrepreneurs to lead and manage business organisations successfully.

A study of business management will help you to understand how business organisations function and how they achieve their objectives. It will also help you to develop and apply skills for learning, skills for life and skills for work.

N5 COURSE CONTENT

The National 5 course comprises three main areas of study:

Understanding Business

This area of study will help you to understand the key objectives of a range of different types of business organisations. It will also enable you to explore a range of factors that relate to the external environment in which an organisation operates, and how these factors impact on the organisation's activities, decision-making and long-term survival.

Management of People and Finance

This area of study will develop a knowledge and understanding of how the management of human resources can contribute to the success of a business organisation. You will find out about the recruitment, selection, training and development and motivation of employees. You will also develop an understanding of how the management of finance is essential for the survival and growth of an organisation, and will analyse the different sources of finance available to business. Finally, you will learn how to prepare financial statements such as cash budgets, income statements and statements of financial position, and break-even analysis calculations.

Management of Marketing and Operations

Marketing can be used to communicate effectively with consumers, maximise customer satisfaction and gain a competitive edge over rival businesses. In this area of the course, you will focus on the key areas of marketing – the marketing mix, product development, the product life cycle and market research. You will also have the opportunity to explore the range of processes and procedures that are used by business organisations to produce different types of goods or services. Finally, you will develop knowledge and understanding of stock management, methods of production and quality control.

COURSE ASSESSMENT STRUCTURE

Question Paper (90 marks)

The question paper gives candidates the opportunity to demonstrate:

- applying knowledge and understanding of relatively complex business concepts
- using data handling techniques to interpret straightforward business information
- evaluating business information to draw conclusions.

The question paper has **90 marks** and represents **75%** of the overall marks for the course assessment.

All questions are mandatory and can cover all areas of the course content.

The question paper has two sections:

Section 1 (40 marks)

Section one consists of two **20-mark** questions based on two pieces of stimulus material. Sub-questions may range in value from 1-5 marks. This area of the question paper assesses decision-making and the application of knowledge and understanding, and can sample course content from any area of the course.

Section 2 (50 marks)

Section two consists of five **10-mark** questions. Sub-questions may range in value from 1-4 marks. This area of the exam paper assesses knowledge and understanding and questions can be drawn from all areas of the course.

The question paper is set and marked externally by the SQA. Candidates complete the paper in 2 hours.

Assignment (30 marks)

The assignment has 30 marks, which represents 25% of the overall marks for the course assessment.

The assignment requires candidates to research and analyse information and prepare a business report. The assignment is:

- set by SQA
- conducted in centres under some supervision and control.

Assignments are submitted to SQA for external marking.

DON'T FORGET

To gain an overall award at National 5 in Business Management, you must secure a pass in **all** of the units as well as in the external course assessments.

HOW THIS BOOK CAN HELP YOU

This *Study Guide* (supported by the Bright Red Digital Zone) explains clearly and concisely all the concepts you need to know and understand to pass the assessments for National 5 Business Management. It also has a wide range of challenging activities, which will develop the following business and entrepreneurial skills:

- numeracy
- research
- presentation skills
- analysing
- employability
- thinking
- planning
- evaluating.
- communication
- decision-making
- creativity
- Information Communications Technology

The new Scottish Curriculum for Excellence advocates providing learners with the opportunity to work independently to develop a deeper understanding of areas of learning that interest them. Throughout this book some extension material has been included to challenge learners and further develop their interest in the subject. Extension material will not be examined by SQA at National 5 level. However, it will be useful for learners who plan to go on and study Business Management at Higher level.

EXAM HINTS

Before you start answering questions in the external examination paper, you should identify the key 'command word' used in each question. This will ensure that you tailor your response to the demands of the question being asked. The table below outlines the key command words which could be used in the final external examination.

Command Word	Meaning
State	Listing or bullet points would be acceptable here.
Suggest	More than just naming or stating. Put forward a recommendation or advise on a possible course of action.
Outline	Identify key features and provide a brief description where appropriate.
Describe	Give a description and use examples where possible as part of the description.
Explain	Give a definition and then an example as to how something may or may not be affected.
Discuss	Give advantages and disadvantages where possible. Use examples to expand your answer, and if possible give a conclusion to your answer.
Justify	You must be able to give reasons why a certain course of action is being taken.

ROLE OF BUSINESS IN SOCIETY 1

SATISFACTION OF HUMAN NEEDS AND WANTS

A business is an organisation that involves people and resources in the making of a good or the provision of a service. All businesses have a name, a set of aims they want to achieve, an image, resources and rules.

As consumers, we buy the goods and services provided by businesses to satisfy our needs and wants.

To survive, we all have basic needs, including:

- food and water
- clothing
- shelter.

Once these needs have been satisfied, people always look for and want more to make their lives more comfortable and enjoyable. For example, we don't **need** a new iPad to survive – we just **want** it because we've seen it advertised, or a friend has one.

DON'T FORGET

Needs and wants are quite different things.

ONLINE

TASK 1: Visit www.brightredbooks.net/N5BusMgmt and find out if you know which item is a need and which item is a want.

PRODUCTION OF GOODS, PROVISION OF SERVICES

Businesses exist to satisfy these needs and wants. Some businesses produce **goods** such as food products, shoes, clothes and electrical goods. Other businesses exist to provide **services** such as transport, hairdressing, banking, fast-food takeaway and holidays.

Goods are **tangible**, which means that they can be seen and physically touched. Services are **intangible**, which means that they cannot be seen or physically touched.

Goods and services can also be **durable** (long-lasting) or **non-durable** (used up quickly).

- A **TV** is an example of a **durable** good – it should last for at least a few years.
- A **cinema** is an example of a **non-durable** service – it provides entertainment in the form of a film for about two to three hours on average. After that, the service is no longer available.

DON'T FORGET

Goods are tangible while services are non-tangible. Goods and services can be durable and non-durable.

ONLINE

TASK 2: Visit www.brightredbooks.net/N5BusMgmt and test your knowledge on goods and services, and whether they are durable or non-durable.

Goods	Services

Cars	Hairdressing
Washing machines	Car servicing
CD players	Insurance
Sweets	Banking
Clothes	Entertainment (for example, cinema and theatre)
Seafood	Education
Shoes	Public transport
Furniture	
Books	

THE BUSINESS CYCLE

The process of buying and selling goods and services is an ongoing one. This is the reason why developing a business is a long-term process, and why many shops, such as Marks and Spencer, Next and New Look, have been on the 'High Street' for a very long time.

This diagram illustrates the process of buying and selling goods and services. It's called the '**business cycle**'.

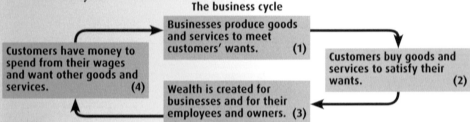

The business cycle

Businesses produce goods and services to meet customers' wants. (1)

Customers buy goods and services to satisfy their wants. (2)

Wealth is created for businesses and for their employees and owners. (3)

Customers have money to spend from their wages and want other goods and services. (4)

Step 1	Entrepreneurs set up in business selling goods and services that consumers need and want.
Step 2	Consumers use their income and go out to the shops and buy goods and services to satisfy their needs and wants.
Step 3	The businesses supplying the goods and services begin to earn **profit** and this means they can pay employees better wages. The owners also become wealthy.
Step 4	Consumers now have even more income to spend (from their wages) and so want even more goods and services.
Step 5	Businesses are now required to expand and produce more goods and services for consumers – and so the **process** goes on.

FACTORS OF PRODUCTION

To make a product or provide a service, you need a number of ingredients or resources – **land, labour, capital** and **enterprise**. These are also referred to as **factors of production**.

Factors of production

LAND	LABOUR
Land means the natural resources that businesses use – for example, a plot of land, coal, forests, water, fields and rivers.	Labour means the workforce of a business – for example, joiners, shop assistants, teachers, clerical staff, electricians and cleaners.
CAPITAL	**ENTERPRISE**
Capital means the tools, machinery and equipment that a business owns – for example, tractors, lorries, motor vehicles, buildings, factories, tools and equipment.	Enterprise means the business ideas that entrepreneurs or owners have about how to use land, labour or capital to make a profit – for example, Richard Branson and Virgin.

 VIDEO LINK

Head to www.brightredbooks.net/N5BusMgmt and check out the 'Factors of production' video for more on this.

 ONLINE TEST

How well have you learned this topic? Take the 'Role of business in society' test at www.brightredbooks.net/N5BusMgmt

 THINGS TO DO AND THINK ABOUT

If you were to make a list of the resources (ingredients) that you need to build a house, your list might include:

wood   bricks   paint   joiners   electricians   cement mixers   ladders   plastic
glass   slates   building company   nails   plot of land   drill   brick layers.

Complete the table below by placing each resource under the appropriate heading.

Land	Labour	Capital	Enterprise

ROLE OF BUSINESS IN SOCIETY 2

ENTERPRISE AND ENTREPRENEURS

An **entrepreneur** is an individual who has the enterprise to develop a business idea by combining the other factors of production – land, labour and capital – to produce a good or provide a service that makes a profit.

Most entrepreneurs begin by setting up a small business that they alone are responsible for managing. However, their role tends to change once the business grows, and they have to employ staff and delegate aspects of their work to other people.

SKILLS AND QUALITIES OF AN ENTREPRENEUR

Entrepreneurs generally have the following skills and qualities. They:

- can identify a **gap in the market**
- are willing to take a risk on a good idea
- have good communication skills
- rise to the challenge and don't give up easily
- have good decision-making skills: they decide which product to produce, the best methods of raising finance, what price to charge customers and which staff to hire
- have good leadership skills: they can lead and motivate their workers to 'achieve the dream'!

IDENTIFYING A GAP IN THE MARKET

One of the key characteristics of an entrepreneur is that they are very good at identifying a gap in the market. This means that they can come up with an idea for a product or service that is not currently being offered by another company, and is not already available in the marketplace.

If an entrepreneur moves quickly to get a product on the market before anyone else, then the financial rewards can be great: customers have to buy from them because nobody else is supplying the product.

The gap in the market might involve providing a product or service in a completely different way. For example, **LoveFilm** rent out DVDs, but they have captured the market from the traditional video shop by providing a more convenient model, where customers receive DVDs through the post, or download them. They also provide customers with a huge list to choose from. Moonpig has done the same with greeting cards.

Businesses use the law to protect their business idea, product or service by registering ownership of the invention and patenting it. They might even sue for damages through the Copyright Act if others try to copy their idea.

They can also register a trademark to make their company stand out from the rest. For example, Nike have trademarked their 'swoosh' logo and their 'just do it' slogan.

ONLINE

TASK 3: Visit www.brightredbooks.net/N5BusMgmt and complete the task on entrepreneurs.

ONLINE

TASK 4: Visit www.brightredbooks.net/N5BusMgmt and create a PowerPoint presentation on two top entrepreneurs.

DON'T FORGET

Spotting a gap in the market is a classic key success factor in business.

SECTORS OF INDUSTRY

Businesses produce different goods and services and belong to different sectors of industry. The three main sectors of industry are classified as follows:

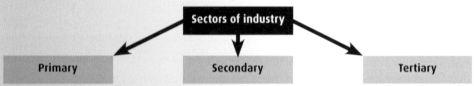

Businesses which exist in the **primary** sector of industry are those concerned with using natural resources such as farming, oil drilling, mining, fishing, and forestry. In other words, these businesses grow products or extract resources from the Earth.

Businesses which exist in the **secondary**, or manufacturing, sector of industry make products. Manufacturing businesses can take the raw materials from businesses in the primary sector and convert them into different products. For example, Kellogg's will purchase crops from farmers to manufacture breakfast cereal. This sector has declined in the UK. Today there are fewer firms who actually manufacture a product.

Businesses which exist in the **tertiary** sector do not produce a product. They provide services like banking, tourism, beauty treatments, hair styling, fitness centres and entertainment, such as film and TV. This sector has increased in the UK. Today there are more businesses that actually provide a service.

SECTORS OF THE ECONOMY

There are three different **sectors of the economy**. These are the private sector, the public sector and the third, or voluntary, sector. The types of business organisation in each of these sectors are listed below:

Private sector
- Sole traders
- Partnerships
- Private limited company (ltd)
- Public limited company (plc)
- Franchise

The main aims of the private sector are to:
- spot a gap in the market
- turn a new idea into a success
- maximise profits.

Public sector
- Central government
- Local government
- Public corporation

The main aims of the public sector are to provide:
- a high quality product/service to all UK citizens
- essential services such as hospital care, education, defence and police
- services that are not entirely profit driven.

Third/voluntary sector
- Charities
- Social clubs and voluntary organisations, for example bowling clubs
- Social enterprises

The main aims of the third/voluntary sector are to:
- raise funds to support causes
- raise awareness, for example, of famine in Africa
- provide services and facilities for members.

While these organisations do not aim to make a profit, they might achieve a surplus of income over expenditure.

THINGS TO DO AND THINK ABOUT

1   Think about the businesses in your area. Identify two businesses that belong to each of the three sectors of industry.

2   Think again about the businesses in your area. Identify two businesses that belong to each of the three sectors of the economy. Which sector does your school belong to?

ONLINE

TASK 5: Visit www.brightredbooks.net/N5BusMgmt and test your knowledge of the sectors of industry.

DON'T FORGET

The sectors of **industry** consist of the primary, secondary and tertiary sectors. The sectors of the **economy** consist of the private, public and third/voluntary sectors.

VIDEO LINK

Head to www.brightredbooks.net/N5BusMgmt and follow the link for some great videos on this topic.

ONLINE

PROGRESS CHECK 1: Visit www.brightredbooks.net/N5BusMgm and test your knowledge of the role of business in society.

ONLINE TEST

How well have you learned this topic? Take the 'Role of business in society' test at www.brightredbooks.net/N5BusMgmt

CUSTOMER SATISFACTION

OVERVIEW

Businesses must meet the needs of their customers if they are to survive. But what do their customers need and want? Here are some key factors:

- good quality products
- attractive packaging
- durability (products that last)
- up-to-date and fashionable products
- good price
- good brand/image
- easily available
- guarantee comes with the product or service
- good after-sales service.

If a business wants to meet the needs of its customers and sell its products or services successfully, it must develop a strategy based on the **four Ps**:

- Product
- Price
- Promotion
- Place.

How these four elements are combined is referred to as **the marketing mix** and will determine how well a product will sell. The following diagram describes the four elements in more detail.

P Product

The good/service that the customer purchases. The total product on offer includes quality, packaging, guarantee and after-sales service.

P Promotion

The way in which the customer is made aware of a product or service, and is persuaded to buy it. Promotion includes advertising, sales and promotions.

MARKETING MIX

P Place

This is where the customer can purchase the good or service – how accessible it is for the customer to buy.

P Price

This is the actual amount paid for the product/service by the customer.

DON'T FORGET

The task for the seller is to **promote** the right **product** at the right **price** in the right **place**!

ONLINE

TASK 6: Visit www. brightredbooks.net/ N5BusMgmt and complete the task on customer service.

WHAT IS CUSTOMER SERVICE?

Customer service is the provision of service to customers **before**, **during** and **after** a purchase. A business should ensure that its customers are dealt with efficiently, consistently and effectively, and it should set up a customer care strategy to do this. This strategy should ensure that there is:

- high quality customer service, with staff who are always happy to help
- a wide range of quality products
- a method for measuring whether customers' needs are being satisfied
- a process for investigating, dealing with and resolving customer complaints to full customer satisfaction.

Many organisations now make customer service a high priority, because it is a lot cheaper to encourage existing customers to keep coming back rather than having to continually advertise to attract new customers.

WHY IS CUSTOMER SERVICE IMPORTANT?

Good customer service has the following long-term benefits for the organisation:
- Good customer relations enhance the organisation's **reputation**. In most customers' minds, the employee and the organisation are one and the same thing, so if the employee has provided good service, then so has the business.
- All organisations benefit from **good publicity** from happy customers. A person with a bad experience is five times more likely to pass on their story than a person with a happy experience.
- Good customer relations are likely to mean **regular repeat orders**. Customers happy with the service they receive are likely to become **loyal customers**.
- Increased loyalty results in more **sales** and a bigger **market share**.
- Good publicity generated by an enhanced reputation means that the company is likely to attract a **better calibre of employees** – people who are looking for a job are attracted first to those businesses with a good reputation.

HOW TO MAXIMISE CUSTOMER SERVICE

Businesses maximise their customer service by:
- keeping customers **well informed** of progress and changes
- **under-promising** and **over-delivering** – they don't set expectations too high, so that customers won't be upset if they aren't met, and they deliver more than customers are expecting, so customers are pleased
- **going the extra mile** to ensure that customers' needs and expectations are always met.

ONLINE

TASK 7: Visit www.brightredbooks.net/N5BusMgmt and fill in the table with the top ten tips for good customer service.

IMPACT OF POOR CUSTOMER SERVICE

Many people will form an opinion of an organisation from the way they are dealt with at their first point of contact with the organisation. Poor customer service can have a very negative impact on a business because:
- It results in bad publicity, as people always tell others about their bad experiences.
- Once a business has a bad reputation, it can be difficult to turn this around: a poor reputation has implications for falling market share and this, in turn, will put customers off.
- Customers who are not happy will not come back. In most cases, people don't complain about their poor service – they just 'vote with their feet' – and this results in falling sales.

ONLINE

TASK 8: Visit www.brightredbooks.net/N5BusMgmt and work with a partner to design a questionnaire.

CASE STUDY

Now would be a great time to check out case study 1 on The Hot Plate. Head to p84, read it through, and answer the questions before checking out the possible solutions on p92.

HOW TO MEASURE CUSTOMER SATISFACTION

Organisations often use **market research** to measure customer satisfaction. They survey customers or ask for feedback to ensure that high standards of customer service are being met, or to find out how they can improve their product or service.

Market research can also help to identify a gap in the market – an idea for a new product or service that customers will want to buy – but we'll look at that in more detail in *Management of Marketing and Operations*. The following methods can be used to check customer satisfaction:
- written survey or questionnaire, which is posted to customers
- telephone call with pre-set questions
- email questionnaire
- meeting, where customers are invited to answer questions and give their opinions
- face-to-face interviews at point-of-sale or on entry to, or exit from, the store
- mystery shoppers, who act as customers to experience the service given by the organisation
- suggestion boxes for customers to leave anonymous suggestions and opinions.

ONLINE

PROGRESS CHECK 2: Visit www.brightredbooks.net/N5BusMgmt and test your knowledge of customer satisfaction.

ONLINE TEST

How well have you learned this topic? Take the 'Customer satisfaction' test at www.brightredbooks.net/N5BusMgmt

THINGS TO DO AND THINK ABOUT

Visit some local businesses, and ask how they measure customer satisfaction.

TYPES OF BUSINESS ORGANISATION 1

OVERVIEW

There are three different sectors of the economy, and there are different types of business within each sector. Here's a quick recap:

Private sector

- Sole trader
- Partnership
- Private limited company (Ltd)
- Public limited company (plc)
- Franchise

Public sector

- Central government
- Local government
- Public corporation

Third/Voluntary sector

- Charities
- Voluntary organisations
- Social enterprises

We'll look at each of these types of business organisation in turn.

PRIVATE SECTOR: SOLE TRADER

A **sole trader** is a one-owner business – in other words, it's owned and controlled by one person. Many small businesses – for example, hairdressers and plumbers – are sole traders.

Sole traders can obtain finance from:

- their own savings
- bank loans
- government grants.

Sole traders usually aim to survive and maximise profits.

Study the following diagram. It outlines some of the features, aims, advantages and disadvantages of being a sole trader.

ONLINE

TASK 9: Visit www.brightredbooks.net/N5BusMgmt and decide whether each point represents a feature, an aim, an advantage or a disadvantage of being a sole trader.

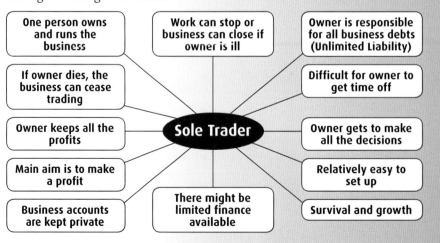

PRIVATE SECTOR: PARTNERSHIP

A **partnership** is a business with two to 20 partners – people who own and control the business together - for example, John Lewis. The partners must produce a Partnership Agreement, which outlines all the rules and conditions that each partner must adhere to. The Agreement also outlines the procedures to be followed when any partner joins, leaves or dies.

Study the following diagram. It outlines some of the features, aims, advantages and disadvantages of forming a Partnership.

VIDEO LINK

Watch the 'Types of business organisations' video at www.brightredbooks.net/N5BusMgmt

ONLINE TEST

How well have you learned this topic? Take the 'Types of business organisation' test at www.brightredbooks.net/N5BusMgmt

THINGS TO DO AND THINK ABOUT

Work in a pair or individually to complete this task.

Decide whether each point represents a feature, an aim, an advantage or a disadvantage of being in a partnership, then complete the table. The first two have been done for you.

Features	Aims	Advantages	Disadvantages
	Survival and growth		Profits have to be shared

TYPES OF BUSINESS ORGANISATION 2

PRIVATE SECTOR: PRIVATE LIMITED COMPANY (LTD)

A **private limited company** has shares that are owned privately – they are not available to the public on the stock market. This type of business can be owned by a family, where all the members of a family are shareholders – for example, Ryanair, Arnold Clark and Baxters Food Group Ltd. There must be at least one director and a secretary, who keeps all the company records. Shareholders have **limited liability,** which means that they can only lose the value of their shares, and not their private assets or belongings.

Study the following diagram. It outlines some of the features, aims, advantages and disadvantages of forming a private limited company.

ONLINE

TASK 10: Visit www.
brightredbooks.net/
N5BusMgmt and decide
whether each point
represents a feature, an
aim, an advantage or a
disadvantage of forming a
private limited company.

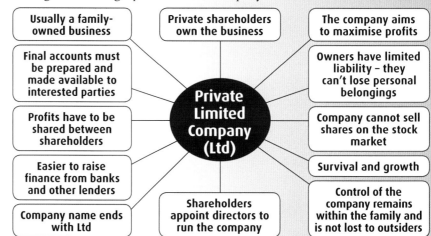

- Usually a family-owned business
- Final accounts must be prepared and made available to interested parties
- Profits have to be shared between shareholders
- Easier to raise finance from banks and other lenders
- Company name ends with Ltd
- Private shareholders own the business
- Shareholders appoint directors to run the company
- **Private Limited Company (Ltd)**
- The company aims to maximise profits
- Owners have limited liability – they can't lose personal belongings
- Company cannot sell shares on the stock market
- Survival and growth
- Control of the company remains within the family and is not lost to outsiders

EXTENSION

This section on public limited
companies and the section
on franchises (p15) are both
extension knowledge which
will be useful if you go on to
study for Higher Business
Management.

PRIVATE SECTOR: PUBLIC LIMITED COMPANY (PLC)

A **public limited company** is a company whose shares are available for purchase by the public on the stock market. There must be a minimum of two shareholders and a minimum of £50000 to start the company. The company is owned by members of the public (shareholders) who appoint a board of directors to manage and control the company on their behalf. Examples of public limited companies are BT, Vodafone, Tesco, Stagecoach and Celtic FC.

Study the following diagram. It outlines some of the features, aims, advantages and disadvantages of forming a public limited company.

ONLINE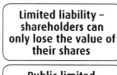

TASK 11: Visit www.
brightredbooks.net/
N5BusMgmt and decide
whether each point
represents a feature, an
aim, an advantage or a
disadvantage of forming a
public limited company.

- Limited liability – shareholders can only lose the value of their shares
- Public limited companies tend to be large
- Survival and growth?
- Owned by shareholders and managed by board of directors
- Name of company ends with the letters plc
- Public limited companies aim to maximise profits
- Members of the public must be able to access all financial records
- **Public Limited Company (plc)**
- Costly and fairly complicated to set up
- They have no control over who buys shares on the stock market
- Easy to borrow huge amounts of money from banks and other lenders
- Members of the public can buy shares in the company on the Stock Exchange
- Can become very powerful and dominant businesses

PRIVATE SECTOR: FRANCHISE

A **franchise** is a business agreement where one business can operate under the name of another business. The **franchisee** pays the **franchisor** a percentage of the annual sales or profits, or agrees to pay a set fee each year. This then allows the franchisee to operate with the business name (which is usually very well known) to sell the products and services associated with that name.

Examples of businesses that operate using the franchise model

Franchisor – this is who owns the original business.

Franchisee – this is who has bought the right to use the original business name and enter into trade, selling its products.

Study the following diagram. It outlines some of the features, aims, advantages and disadvantages of operating as a franchise.

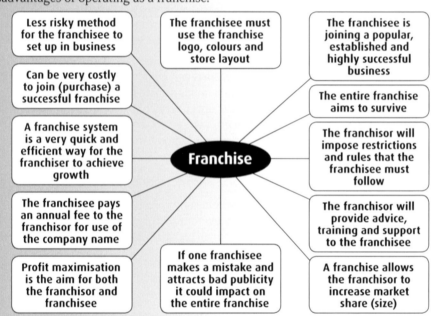

- Less risky method for the franchisee to set up in business
- Can be very costly to join (purchase) a successful franchise
- A franchise system is a very quick and efficient way for the franchiser to achieve growth
- The franchisee pays an annual fee to the franchisor for use of the company name
- Profit maximisation is the aim for both the franchisor and franchisee
- The franchisee must use the franchise logo, colours and store layout
- If one franchisee makes a mistake and attracts bad publicity it could impact on the entire franchise
- The franchisee is joining a popular, established and highly successful business
- The entire franchise aims to survive
- The franchisor will impose restrictions and rules that the franchisee must follow
- The franchisor will provide advice, training and support to the franchisee
- A franchise allows the franchisor to increase market share (size)

Franchise

THINGS TO DO AND THINK ABOUT

The table below sets out keywords and their definitions for companies in the private sector. Discuss them with other people in your class, and remember them.

Key word	Meaning
Stock Market	Where people buy and sell shares in companies – this is now mainly done online.
Limited Liability	Investors in a business (company) can only lose the value of the shares they own – their private belongings cannot be taken to pay the company's debts.
Companies Act	An act of law which sets out the rules and procedures by which companies must abide.
Shareholders	People who invest (use their own money) to buy shares in a company. Shareholders jointly own the company.
Board of Directors	A group of highly skilled and professional managers who are appointed by the shareholders (owners) to run the company on their behalf.
Annual Accounts	Statements that are produced once per year and show the value of the business's assets and how much profit the business has made in the current year.

ONLINE

TASK 12: Visit www.brightredbooks.net/N5BusMgmt and decide whether each point represents a feature, an aim, an advantage or a disadvantage of operating as a franchise.

CASE STUDY

Turn to p84, read case study 2, on 'Delivering fast food franchising', before checking out the possible solutions on p92.

DON'T FORGET

The private sector is made up of the following types of business organisations who operate with the main aim of earning profit:
- Sole traders
- Partnerships
- Private limited companies
- Public limited companies
- Franchises

It is important that you do not confuse public limited companies with the public sector!

ONLINE

PROGRESS CHECK 3: Visit www.brightredbooks.net/N5BusMgmt and test your knowledge of businesses that operate in the private sector.

ONLINE TEST

How well have you learned this topic? Take the 'Types of business organisation' test at www.brightredbooks.net/N5BusMgmt

TYPES OF BUSINESS ORGANISATION 3

DON'T FORGET

To achieve its aims and objectives, central government delegates resources and responsibility to local government.

PUBLIC SECTOR: LOCAL GOVERNMENT

Local government (councils) are set up by central government (Scottish Parliament) and are run on its behalf by locally-elected councillors. The day-to-day running of services is organised by managers and employees from each council.

A local council aims to meet the needs of local people and businesses. It is required to provide the most efficient service possible within allocated budgets, rather than to make a profit.

Functions

Local government's functions include:

- **education and leisure services:** staffing; buildings; museums; pools and sports centres; childcare; psychological services; halls and community facilities and libraries
- **social work:** community care; children and family services
- **planning and transport:** roads, public transport, economic development; flood prevention; development of new buildings
- **environmental services:** refuse collection and disposal; street lighting; food safety; health promotion; animal welfare; maintenance of parks and cemeteries
- **housing:** allocation and maintenance of public housing; homeless provision; rent collection; building new council houses
- **finance:** annual budgets for managing income and spending; financial reports; collection of Council Tax and business rates
- **information technology:** use of ICT across all council services.

The work of local government obviously has a huge impact on the lives of local residents. However, local governments generally have to act within central government policy, even if they don't agree with it.

Local government activities are constantly monitored to ensure that they are always achieving 'best value'.

Finance

Local government is financed in a variety of ways including by:

- **government grants:** the main source of local government income. This money comes from the UK government via the Scottish Parliament, and accounts for about 40 per cent of total council income
- **council tax:** the amount of money paid by each household, based on the value of the property. Each local authority sets its own council tax rate
- **non-domestic rates:** payments by businesses which are set by the central government and are the same across the country; charges for services such as entrance to leisure facilities; housing rents
- **the sale of assets:** for example, council houses.

ONLINE

TASK 13 Visit www.brightredbooks.net/N5BusMgmt for a task about the public sector.

THIRD/VOLUNTARY SECTOR: OVERVIEW

Organisations in the **third** or **voluntary sector** have different aims from those in the private and public sectors. They are 'not for profit' organisations, and their reason for existing is usually to help a charitable cause in some way.

CHARITIES

The government regulates the activities of **charities** and keeps a Register of Charities in the UK. Charities are exempt from paying most taxes. They are often set up as trusts with no individual owner, and overall management and control is undertaken by unpaid trustees – people who are placed in a position of trust with the responsibility of looking after the interests of others.

Aims and objectives

Charities' aims and objectives are to:

- provide a service
- relieve poverty
- fund medical research
- provide protection to the vulnerable.

Finance

Charities are financed in a variety of ways:

- donations from the public
- donations from companies
- government grants
- lottery grants
- profits from charity shops.

 ONLINE

TASK 14: Visit www. brightredbooks.net/ N5BusMgmt, carry out the required research and create a PowerPoint presentation.

VOLUNTARY ORGANISATIONS

Voluntary organisations are run and staffed by volunteers. Examples include the Scouts, youth clubs, Brownies and sports clubs. They bring together people with similar interests. They are run by a committee of elected volunteers.

These organisations can raise finance by applying for grants from the lottery, Sports Council or local authorities. They can also charge a fee if people want to become a member of their organisation or use their facilities.

 ONLINE

PROGRESS CHECK 4: Visit www.brightredbooks.net/ N5BusMgmt and test your knowledge of businesses that operate in the public and third/voluntary sectors.

SOCIAL ENTERPRISES

A **social enterprise** is a business that has a social and/or an environmental purpose. It has a clear sense of its social mission. There are many different types of social enterprise. Examples include The Big Issue, the Eden Project and Jamie Oliver's restaurant Fifteen.

Aims and objectives

A social enterprise's aims and objectives are to:

- have a clear social, and/or environmental mission
- generate the majority of their income through trade – buying and selling
- reinvest the majority of their profits in their social mission
- be independent from state intervention
- be majority controlled, in the interest of the social mission
- be accountable and transparent.

Finance

Social enterprises are financed in a variety of ways:

- **grants**
- **loans**
- **crowd funding**: a large number of people each give a small amount of money to fund a project.
- **equity finance**: this involves the exchange of capital for part-ownership of the business as in, for example, Dragon's Den. The two main providers of equity finance are venture capitalists and business angels.
- **community finance**: this is often provided by Community Development Finance Institutions and Credit Unions

 ONLINE TEST

How well have you learned this topic? Take the 'Types of business organisation' test at www.brightredbooks.net/ N5BusMgmt

 THINGS TO DO AND THINK ABOUT

Find out if there are any social enterprises in your area. If there are, go and talk to them about what they do. If there aren't, visit www.socialenterprise.org.uk and undertake some research about the types of social enterprise that already exist.

BUSINESS OBJECTIVES

UNDERSTANDING BUSINESS OBJECTIVES

Businesses have a number of key objectives. These are outlined in the following diagram:

Sales maximisation

The business aims to achieve as much sales revenue as possible. This is popular with sales staff who might receive bonuses or salaries according to the number of sales made.

Customer satisfaction

High standards of customer satisfaction ensure customer loyalty. It is easier for a business to retain existing customers rather than continually attract new customers.

Provision of a service

A charity or local authority (council) would have this objective.

Profit maximisation

Most private sector organisations – for example, sole trader, partnership, limited company or public limited company – aim to make as much profit as possible.

Key Business Objectives

Survival

Continuing to stay in business is vital, especially for a new business. It can be difficult to survive in hard times, for example, when the country is in recession and consumers have little money to spend.

Growth

Many organisations aim to grow from a small business into a large business. A large firm can be more competitive, earn more profit and can also reduce the risk of failure.

Social responsibility

Many organisations aim to have a good image and take responsibility for the environment, for example, reducing pollution and investing in recycling and other environmentally friendly issues.

Market share and enterprise

Some business organisations aim to increase their share of the market in an attempt to stay ahead of their competitors or, indeed, to remove their competitors from the market.

Developing new ideas and products to satisfy consumer wants enables businesses to be seen as innovative market leaders.

Managerial objectives

Sometimes managers have their own objectives – for example, to increase their own salaries or to enter into business contracts with particular customers or clients.

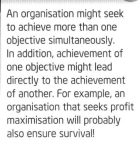

DON'T FORGET

An organisation might seek to achieve more than one objective simultaneously. In addition, achievement of one objective might lead directly to the achievement of another. For example, an organisation that seeks profit maximisation will probably also ensure survival!

THINGS TO DO AND THINK ABOUT

Read the following case study and then answer the questions that follow.

McDonald's logo

McDonald's has proudly run its business in the UK since 1974 and currently operates more than 1200 restaurants across Britain and Ireland.

Above all, serving quality food that our customers can trust is McDonald's number one priority. But McDonald's is about more than just the number of restaurants we operate. It's about our suppliers, franchisees and employees working together. It's about the investment we are making together in our restaurants and in our 97 000 employees. It's about the skills and opportunities we offer and the ways in which we support our local communities.

We are a proud supporter of British agriculture. We source the majority of our ingredients from around 17 500 British and Irish farms.

We employ over 97 000 employees and invest over £43 million every year on training and development. We offer our people clear career progression; in fact nine out of ten restaurant managers and one in five franchisees started as crew. Around 70 per cent of our restaurants in the UK are owned and operated by local businessmen and women.

Our restaurants are very much part of the local community – we lead and support a range of community activities from litter-picking patrols to charity events and local football matches. In fact, we have a long tradition of supporting community football; for over ten years we have supported initiatives to encourage young people into football through helping to train coaches and volunteers for local clubs.

1 What sector of industry does McDonald's operate in?

2 What is the main priority of McDonald's other than profit and market growth?

3 McDonald's aims to be socially responsible. Describe how McDonald's aims to serve the local community.

ONLINE

PROGRESS CHECK 5: Visit www.brightredbooks.net/ N5BusMgmt and test your knowledge of business objectives.

ONLINE TEST

How well have you learned this topic? Take the 'Business objectives' test at www.brightredbooks.net/ N5BusMgmt

EXTERNAL AND INTERNAL FACTORS

EXTERNAL FACTORS

There are a number of key factors in the external environment of a business. All businesses must react efficiently to changes in their external environment – if they don't, the business could fail. **External factors** can be summarised as follows.

P	**Political Factors**
E	**Economic Factors**
S	**Social Factors**
T	**Technological Factors**
E	**Environmental Factors**
C	**Competitive Factors**

DON'T FORGET

Use the PESTEC acronym to help you remember the six key external factors that affect a business.

CASE STUDY

Turn to pp86–87 for case studies 3, 4 and 5 on Ratcliffe Food, Scott's Pics and Christmas deliveries.

Political

The government can introduce laws which could affect every business in the UK. For example, the government passed laws to ban advertising tobacco on television. Businesses must comply with laws or face heavy legal penalties.

The government can also affect businesses by changing the amount of corporation tax charged on business profits. It has also introduced a minimum wage which employers must pay – this will affect their costs and profits.

Economic

If there is a recession and unemployment is high, consumers will have less income, which will result in a loss of sales for businesses. Businesses might have to 'slash' prices to encourage customers to keep buying from them. This will mean a cut in profits but they will have to accept this if they are to survive.

Social

There have been changes in the population structure of the UK. More people are living longer and so the elderly are now making up a larger percentage of the total population. Business must take note of this and produce goods and services relevant to the needs of the population.

Technological

To succeed, businesses must keep up with changes in technology. For example, they must become involved in e-commerce – buying and selling goods using the internet. They must also use technology and robots in production lines when manufacturing their products. Failure to keep up with technology could lead to a fall in sales and profits.

Environmental

There is now increasing pressure for firms to be environmentally friendly. For example, many firms have introduced 'bags for life' to encourage people to stop using plastic carrier bags.

Businesses can also be seriously disrupted by extreme weather conditions like storms, floods and snow.

Competitive

All businesses face competition from other firms, both in the UK and abroad. For example, when the National Lottery was launched, Littlewoods Pools had to change the way they advertised to compete with the Lottery.

INTERNAL FACTORS

There are a number of key factors in the internal environment of a business that can have an impact on how successful it is. These are finance, staff, management, information and technology.

Finance

Finance is crucial. A lack of money could mean that a business has to consider cost cutting measures such as staff redundancies or closing branches of the business.

Changes in costs, such as wage rises or increases in the cost of stock, could mean that the business has to take a cut in profits.

Staff

Expert and capable staff will be more productive in their work and will help the business to achieve more.

Management

A strong and capable management team will make good decisions – and this, in turn, will lead the business to success.

Information

A business needs to carry out thorough market research to obtain accurate information about its customers and what they need and want.

Technology

The use of ICT and robots means that goods or services can be produced more efficiently and more cost-effectively.

DON'T FORGET

The five key internal factors that affect a business are finance, staff, management, information and technology.

ONLINE

PROGRESS CHECK 6: Visit www.brightredbooks.net/N5BusMgmt and test your knowledge of the key external and internal factors that impact on businesses.

ONLINE TEST

How well have you learned this topic? Take the 'Internal and external factors' test at www.brightredbooks.net/N5BusMgmt

THINGS TO DO AND THINK ABOUT

Below are three very well-known businesses.

1   2   3

For business number 1, identify one factor in its **social external environment** that could pose a problem.

For business number 2, identify one factor in its **competitive external environment** that could pose a problem.

For business number 3, identify one factor in its **economic external environment** that could pose a problem.

STAKEHOLDERS

The definition of **stakeholders** is 'a person or a group of people who have an interest in a business or organisation and in the way in which it is managed and run'.

 ACTIVITY

Think about your school. Complete the diagram by adding the stakeholders who have an interest in your school, and what those interests are. The first two have been done for you.

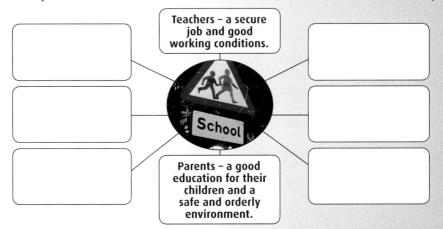

Teachers – a secure job and good working conditions.

School

Parents – a good education for their children and a safe and orderly environment.

Once you've completed this activity, you'll understand that there are many people or stakeholders who are concerned with the welfare of your school.

Similarly, in every business organisation – from large companies like British Airways to your local corner shop – there are a number of people or stakeholders who expect that business to produce results that suit their needs.

ONLINE TEST

How well have you learned this topic? Take the 'Stakeholders' test at www.brightredbooks.net/N5BusMgmt

DON'T FORGET

Competitors are not a stakeholder! They have absolutely no interest in an organisation other than wanting it to fail as a way of removing competition.

DON'T FORGET

All stakeholders have different interests in an organisation and are able to influence an organisation in many different ways.

ONLINE

TASKS 15, 16 and 17: Visit www.brightredbooks.net/N5BusMgmt and complete the tasks on stakeholders.

INTERNAL AND EXTERNAL STAKEHOLDERS

Some stakeholders (such as staff) are actually in the business and are called **internal stakeholders**, while others (such as customers) are outwith the business and are called **external stakeholders**. Below are some of the more common business stakeholders, along with their specific interests.

Stakeholder	Interests
Owners	The owners have invested their own money, time and effort in the business. They want it to thrive and grow and make a profit.
Shareholders	Shareholders have bought shares in the public limited company, and they want a good return on the money they have invested through the payment of dividends. They also want to see the value of their shares rise.
Employees	Employees want job security, to be paid a fair wage and to be part of a successful, thriving business.
Managers	Managers are employed by the business and will sometimes have special arrangements in place that will entitle them to additional pay (a bonus) if the business if performing well. On the other hand, if the business is **not** doing well they could possibly be sacked. A good example of this is when a football team gets bad results: the team's manager is normally the person who is 'given the axe'.
Suppliers	Suppliers need to be guaranteed that if they supply the goods on **credit** to the business, then the company has the ability to pay them back.
Customers	The customers of a business want the business to provide them with a quality product or service at an affordable and reasonable price.

contd

Support agencies	Support agencies provide support and advice for entrepreneurs and start-up businesses. These include Business Gateway and the Prince's Scottish Youth Business Trust. It is important that the people and businesses they help out do well, so that they become well-respected within the business community and continue to provide the services they offer.
Central government	Central government – in the form of the Inland Revenue (HMRC) – needs to know how successful the business is to ensure that they collect and receive the correct amount of tax.
Banks	Banks want to make sure that if they provide an organisation with a loan, the organisation will be able to pay it back within the terms and conditions of the loan agreement.
Local community	The local community wants the business to do well, so it can provide employment in the area, and support local projects. The community also wants to ensure that the business doesn't create any negative effects such as pollution or traffic congestion.

For stakeholders to have power and influence, their **desire** to exert influence must be combined with their **ability** to exert influence on the business.

Stakeholder	Influence
Managers	They can decide on staffing levels and what new products the business will introduce.
Employees	Employees can take industrial action, for example, strike, if they are unhappy with working conditions.
Customers	If customers are not happy with the service offered by the business, they can go elsewhere, for example, to a rival business.
Suppliers	Suppliers can change prices, credit arrangements and discount rates at short notice.
Lenders	Lenders can withhold the offer of a loan change interest rates to be paid on loans.
Local Community/Pressure Groups	Can protest and raise awareness if a business is polluting or damaging the environment.

DISAGREEMENTS BETWEEN STAKEHOLDERS

Due to the demands placed on businesses by so many different stakeholders, conflicts can arise between the different groups. Some of the more common areas of conflict are:

Shareholders and management
Profit maximisation is often the most important objective of shareholders – resulting in large dividend payments for them. However, it is far more likely that the Sales Manager, for example, will aim to maximise sales rather than profit to earn high bonuses.

Customers and the business
Customers are unlikely to remain loyal and repeat purchase from the business if the product is of poor quality and/or is poor value for money. However, owners of the business could attempt to cut costs to maximise profits, which results in poorer quality products.

Suppliers and the business
Many suppliers complain that businesses take too long to pay for raw materials that have already been delivered to them and, as a result, they sometimes refuse to sell on credit. Many businesses, on the other hand, have been known to complain that raw materials are delivered late and are of poor quality.

The community and the business
A large company can sometimes have a negative impact on the local community through, for example, pollution, noise, congestion and the siting of new factories in areas of outstanding beauty. Strong protest from local residents and pressure groups can mean that the business decides to relocate to another area, although this can create unemployment in the community it leaves behind.

 CASE STUDY

Head to pp88-9 for case studies 6, 7 and 8 on Thomson Holidays, Howsters and Asda.

 ONLINE

PROGRESS CHECK 7: Visit www.brightredbooks.net/N5BusMgmt and test your knowledge of the different types of stakeholders and their interests.

 EXTENSION

This section on disagreements between stakeholders is extension knowledge which will be useful if you go on to study for Higher Business Management and the section on disagreements between the community and business commonly features in exam questions at this level.

 THINGS TO DO AND THINK ABOUT

Go through each of the stakeholders discussed in this section again, and identify which is an internal stakeholder, and which is an external stakeholder.

RECRUITMENT AND SELECTION 1

THE ROLE OF HUMAN RESOURCE MANAGEMENT

Human Resource Management (HRM) refers to the function within an organisation that recruits, trains, develops and maintains an effective workforce.

No matter the size or objectives of an organisation, the most valuable resource it possesses is its workforce. Without workers who are both efficient and effective, the organisation is unlikely to achieve long-term success. The human resources of an organisation comprise its entire workforce – from the managing director to the part-time cleaner. Each person is employed to perform specific tasks which play their part in the overall success or failure of an organisation.

Human Resource Management is therefore about getting the right people in the right place at the right time. Human Resource Management can be split into four main areas:

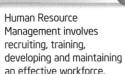

DON'T FORGET

Human Resource Management involves recruiting, training, developing and maintaining an effective workforce.

Recruitment and selection of staff	Retaining and motivating staff
HUMAN RESOURCE MANAGEMENT (HRM)	
Training and staff development	Employment legislation

EXTENSION

This section on internal versus external recruitment is extension knowledge which will be useful if you go on to study for Higher Business Management.

METHODS OF RECRUITMENT

When a vacancy arises within an organisation, the position can be filled **internally** or **externally**. People usually leave their positions for one of four reasons:

- they've got a promotion
- they've got a job with another organisation
- they've been sacked
- they're retiring or taking a career break due to personal circumstances.

Internal recruitment looks for suitable candidates from staff who already work for the organisation. The new job could offer them a chance to move departments or gain promotion with more responsibility. These posts can be advertised on notice boards within the business or on the company intranet.

External recruitment looks for suitable candidates outside the organisation. The job might be advertised in the press, in job centres or on websites – anywhere where lots of people are likely to see it.

contd

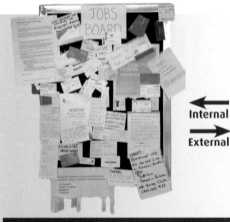

Internal ←

External →

Advantages of internal recruitment	Advantages of external recruitment
The person is already known to the organisation and so there is less chance of appointing the 'wrong' person.	There is a wider pool of candidates to select from, and therefore a better opportunity to select the best candidate for the vacancy.
It is cheaper – the cost of advertising, for example in newspapers, can be avoided.	Staff appointed from outside the organisation can bring new skills and ideas to the organisation.
The opportunity to gain promotion within an organisation can motivate employees.	Workers who have already been trained by other organisations can be attracted to the business, and so there will be a saving on training costs.
If the organisation has spent time and money training a member of staff, this will not be lost if an employee has to leave an organisation to gain promotion.	There is an opportunity to 'head hunt' candidates with a proven track record.

There are a number of methods that can be used for recruiting staff from outside the organisation:

- job centres
- newspapers
- employment agencies
- trade magazines
- internet
- schools, colleges and universities.

 **ACTIVITY**

In the video clip 'How can recruitment affect a business?' (available at www. brightredbooks.net/N5BusMgmt), a group of business experts (including Lord Sugar) explain what they look for in general when they are recruiting an employee, and Hugh Pym explains why companies have recruitment policies. Take notes while you are watching this. Keep these points in the back of your mind when you go onto the next section about the recruitment and selection process.

 THINGS TO DO AND THINK ABOUT

Write to a local business, and ask their Human Resources Management Department about their recruitment policy. Do they tend to recruit staff internally or externally, or do they use a mixture of both? Ask to see a copy of their policy, if they have one.

RECRUITMENT AND SELECTION 2

ONLINE

TASK 18: Visit www.
brightredbooks.net/
N5BusMgmt and complete a
person specification for the
job vacancy.

ONLINE

TASK 19: Visit www.
brightredbooks.net/
N5BusMgmt and answer
the questions about the job
description.

DON'T FORGET

Wage costs are one of the
biggest expenses a business
has to pay, and paying wages
unnecessarily will lead to
reduced profits.

THE RECRUITMENT AND SELECTION PROCESS

The recruitment and selection process begins when there is a vacancy in the
organisation that needs to be filled. This process has the following steps:

Step 1 – Prepare **job analysis**
Step 2 – Prepare **job specification/description**
Step 3 – Prepare **person specification**
Step 4 – **Advertise** job
Step 5 – Issue **application forms** and/or **request CVs**
Step 6 – **Receive** applications
Step 7 – **Shortlist** candidates
Step 8 – **Hold interviews**
Step 9 – **Offer** the **position**

Steps 1 to 5 deal with recruitment. Steps 6 to 9 deal with selection.

THE RECRUITMENT PROCESS

The recruitment process consists of the first five steps from above. We'll look at each of
these steps in turn.

Prepare job analysis

Preparing a **job analysis** is the first stage in the recruitment process – and possibly the
most important one. When an employee leaves the organisation, it might be that their work
could be shared among the remaining employees or that their role is no longer needed. If
so, there is no need to fill the vacancy or to carry on paying wages unnecessarily.

Prepare job specification/description

If the job analysis results in the identification of a vacancy, then a **job specification/
description** must be drawn up. This lists all of the duties that will be involved in the role:

- job title
- pay
- holiday entitlement
- line manager
- any decision-making powers the employee will have.
- location of work
- hours of work
- conditions of work
- duties and responsibilities

The job specification/description will then be used to produce an advertisement for the job.

Experience

Education

Training

Prepare person specification

A **person specification** will outline the skills,
qualifications, experience and qualities that the ideal
candidate should possess. Examples could be, 'must hold
a university degree' or 'must be able to work as part of a
team'. It should include:

- experience (essential or preferred)
- education and qualifications
- character and personality
- soft skills (team player, leader etc.)
- special skills required
- training.

An example of a person specification is shown on
page 27.

contd

PERSON SPECIFICATION FOR A JUNIOR ADMINISTRATIVE ASSISTANT		
Criteria	**Essential**	**Desirable**
Skills, knowledge and abilities	Ability to accurately key in data. Ability to create and edit word-processed documents. Ability to create and edit spreadsheets. Ability to use email and internet confidently. Ability to file accurately. Ability to deal with visitors to the organisation.	Ability to create and edit databases. Ability to **prioritise** workloads in order to meet deadlines. Ability to learn new ICT skills quickly. Ability to work on own **initiative**.
Qualifications	National 5 Administration & IT or equivalent.	N5 English, Maths, Administration & IT or Business Management.
Experience		Previous work experience at junior administrative level.
Personal qualities	Excellent verbal and written communication skills, including good telephone manner. Ability to quickly follow verbal and written instructions. Willingness to undertake training to improve skills.	Good organisation skills. Good time management skills.

Advertise job

The Human Resources Department will then need to write an advertisement for the job and place it in a variety of media such as those listed on p 25. The aim is to get as many people as possible to apply for the vacant position. The advertisement will include:

- job title
- hours of work
- pay and fringe benefits
- relevant experience and qualifications required
- name and address of person that prospective applicants should contact.

It is likely that the job will be advertised internally within the business as well as through external media. The advantages of recruiting from within the existing workforce include the fact that a shorter training and induction period is necessary, as well as less time and money being spent on the whole process.

Issue application forms and/or request CVs

The Human Resources Department then sends out application forms to, and/or requests **Curriculum Vitae** (CVs) from, all those people who have asked to apply for the vacant job.

It is important that the application form is tailored to the specific post that is being advertised, as well as asking questions that are relevant, legal, inoffensive and essential.

All application forms should contain basic information such as:
- name, address, telephone number
- education and qualifications
- work experience
- interests, hobbies
- referees (names and addresses of people who will supply a reference about the job applicant.

Curriculum Vitae means 'life history'. CVs are prepared by most job applicants and provide a short summary of the applicant's career achievements to date. Some businesses might ask applicants to send a copy of their CV together with a letter of application, instead of an application form. There's an example of a completed Standard Application Form for the position of Junior Store Person on the Digital Zone.

THINGS TO DO AND THINK ABOUT

Study the person specification for the Junior Administrative Assistant and then discuss the following questions with a partner.

1 Explain the difference between essential and desirable criteria.

2 Using the person specification for Marks and Spencer on the Digital Zone, identify two skills that are essential for job applicants to have.

3 Identify two qualifications that are desirable but not essential in prospective job applicants.

4 Identify two personal qualities that are essential for all prospective job applicants to have.

ONLINE

TASK 20: Visit www.brightredbooks.net/N5BusMgmt and draw up a person specification and a job description.

ONLINE

TASK 21: Visit www.brightredbooks.net/N5BusMgmt and prepare an advertisement for the post of English teacher at your school.

ONLINE

TASK 22: Visit www.brightredbooks.net/N5BusMgmt and fill in an application form for a job.

ONLINE

TASK 23: Visit www.brightredbooks.net/N5BusMgmt and write your own CV.

ONLINE

PROGRESS CHECK 9: Visit www.brightredbooks.net/N5BusMgmt and test your knowledge of the recruitment process.

ONLINE TEST

How well have you learned this topic? Take the 'Recruitment process' test at www.brightredbooks.net/N5BusMgmt

RECRUITMENT AND SELECTION 3

THE SELECTION PROCESS

The selection process consists of the following four steps.

Step 6   Receive applications
Step 7   Shortlist candidates
Step 8   Hold interviews
Step 9   Offer the position

We'll look at each of these steps in turn.

Receive applications

Once the application forms have been completed and returned to the business (usually with a CV and a covering letter) then the short-listing process will begin.

Shortlist candidates

In the current climate of high unemployment, it's very likely that the advertised vacancy will produce many application forms or CVs. It wouldn't be practical to interview everyone who applies for the job, so a 'shortlist' of the most suitable candidates is drawn up.

The HR Department will compare the application forms and/or CVs received to the job description and person specification to determine which appear to match. This will determine which applicants make it on to the short list to be interviewed.

Hold interviews

One-to-one interview

Panel interview

contd

Group interview

Interviews are the most common way to select the successful candidate.

Interviews can be done face-to-face, over the phone or by videoconferencing.

Interview formats can be:

- one-to-one – where one individual interviews one candidate
- a panel – where a group of people interviews one candidate
- group – where a group of people interviews a group of candidates.

The interview process is very time-consuming, but it is an essential factor in getting the 'right' person appointed to the job.

The interview can range from being totally **unstructured,** to being completely **structured** (or carefully designed beforehand).

The most **structured interviews** have characteristics such as standardised questions, trained interviewers, specific question order, controlled length of time and a standardised response evaluation format.

A completely **unstructured interview** would probably be done 'off the cuff' with untrained interviewers, random questions and with no consideration of time.

Good interviewers will bring out the best in each candidate by being open-minded and unbiased. Candidates should be made to feel welcome and relaxed and the interviewer should control the interview to ensure that all the relevant information is gained and given.

Some applicants, however, might be highly experienced at interviews, especially if they have applied for many jobs in the past. In this situation, they could convince the interviewer that they have the ideal skills and abilities for the job, when they don't.

Because of this problem, other selection strategies or methods of assessment have been devised to assist in the recruitment process. We'll look at these in the next section.

ONLINE

PROGRESS CHECK 10: Visit www.brightredbooks.net/ N5BusMgmt and test your knowledge of the selection process.

ONLINE TEST

How well have you learned this topic? Take the 'Selection process' test at www.brightredbooks.net/ N5BusMgmt

THINGS TO DO AND THINK ABOUT

With a partner, role play being an inteviewer and an interviewee.

RECRUITMENT AND SELECTION 4

METHODS OF ASSESSMENT

The following methods of assessment are often used – alongside an interview – to select the successful candidate.

Knowledge tests

These tests involve specific questions to determine how much the individual knows about particular job tasks and responsibilities. Traditionally, they have been administered in a paper-and-pencil format, but testing on computer is becoming more common. Banks sometimes use these tests to help them decide who to interview.

Work-sample or performance tests

These require the individual to actually demonstrate or perform one or more job tasks. These tests generally show a high degree of job-relatedness. For example, an applicant for an office-machine repairman position might be asked to diagnose the problem with a malfunctioning machine – and could indeed be asked to repair it.

Assessment centres

Candidates are generally assessed in these centres in a variety of ways, including interviews, ability tests, personality measures and a range of management activities and problem-solving exercises such as the following:

'In-basket' tasks – where candidates are asked to look through a manager's 'in-basket' of letters, memos, mail, and reports. These contain a number of problems that have to be addressed. Candidates are then asked to examine them, prioritise them and respond appropriately with problem-solving strategies.

Role-play exercises – where candidates are asked to pretend that they already have the job and must interact with another employee to solve a given problem. The other employee is usually a trained assessor.

Leaderless tasks – where a group of candidates are asked to respond to various problems and challenges, without a designated group leader. Candidates are evaluated on their behaviour in the group discussions. This could include their teamwork skills, their interaction with others or their leadership skills.

Trained assessors rate how well each candidate performs.

Aptitude tests

These tests measure how good the applicant is at a particular skill, for example, mathematical skills, keyboard skills, shorthand speeds or driving ability.

Psychometric tests

These tests are designed to measure the intellectual ability, personality, attitudes and character of the applicant. These are usually timed, multiple-choice tests, taken under exam conditions.

Personality tests

These aim to determine whether the applicant is a team player or not, and what team role or roles they perform best – for example, are they a team leader, or do they contribute specialist skills to a team?

Physical ability tests

Physical ability tests – often used by the police, fire brigade and army – focus on testing strength, endurance and physical speed and coordination.

OFFER THE POSITION

Only one applicant can be successful. Once the interviewers and/or assessors come to an agreement, one of the candidates will be offered the position – either by telephone, letter or email – subject to satisfactory **reference checks**. A starting date will be agreed. Once the candidate has accepted the offer, they should receive a Contract of Employment within two months. The Contract of Employment outlines:

- title of job, hours of work and holiday entitlement
- rate and timing of payment of wage or salary
- sickness pay and allowances
- pension scheme
- disciplinary procedures
- notice required if employee intends to give up the job.

REFERENCE CHECKS

Once the successful candidate has been chosen, HRM will use **reference checks** to verify or make sure that the information provided by the candidate about their education, employment history and achievements is correct.

Reference checks aren't used as a way of separating good workers from poor workers, because they almost always result in positive reports. Their purpose is to give applicants the incentive to be honest with the information they provide.

ONLINE TEST

How well have you learned this topic? Take the 'Recruitment and selection test' at www.brightredbooks. net/NBusMgmt

THINGS TO DO AND THINK ABOUT

You might come across some of these assessment methods while applying for a job in the future, so have a go and see how you get on!

Aptitude test

Candidates applying for office work might be asked to take an aptitude test to measure the accuracy and speed of their keyboard skills.

Visit the website www.typeonline.co.uk/copypractice.php

Don't complete the copy practice test. Have a few attempts at the test and then note your accuracy and speed.

On a sheet of A4 paper, write a short paragraph to explain how an aptitude test could help an employer to select the best candidate for a job.

Psychometric test

A manager applying for a senior position in an organisation might be asked to undertake a psychometric test to assess their intellectual ability, character, personality and attitudes.

Visit the website www.psychometricinstitute. co.uk/Free-Personality-Test.asp

Complete the psychometric test.

On a sheet of A4 paper, write a short paragraph to explain how a psychometric test could help an employer select the best candidate for a job.

TRAINING 1

ONLINE

PROGRESS CHECK 11: Visit www.brightredbooks.net/N5BusMgmt and test your knowledge of the selection process.

Staff training

THE ROLE OF TRAINING

Employees learn how to do their job – or how to do their job more efficiently – through the process of staff training.

Once a new employee has been appointed, they will probably receive **induction training** to help them settle into the new job and into the organisation. This induction training will probably include:

- a tour of the premises and its facilities – including, for example, the canteen and toilets
- an introduction to other employees
- an explanation of company policies – for example, absence procedures
- health and safety training – for example, what to do in a fire
- information about how to carry out the role and the day-to-day duties involved in the job
- background information about the organisation – for example, its business objectives.

However, training is not limited to the new employees of a business. Training courses are likely to be targeted at all employees at various stages in their career and can range from management training courses to training on how to use new machinery and technology.

There are many reasons for the extensive use of training across the workforce. It can:

1 improve employee productivity
2 create a multi-skilled, flexible workforce
3 increase the levels of job satisfaction and motivation of the employees
4 increase employees' chances of promotion.

HOW DOES AN ORGANISATION PLAN SUITABLE TRAINING?

An organisation can plan suitable training by undertaking a **skill scan.** This is a document that is completed by the employee and the employer. It allows both parties to consider the strengths and any weaknesses in the employee's performance, and to compare each other's views of the work being done.

Skill scans are often completed at, or prior to, an annual appraisal with the employee's line manager and aim to:
- assess the employee's current skills
- set realistic targets for their future development and identify ways to achieve them – for example, through training
- review the targets to see what progress the employee has made.

This process should help employees stay motivated and can lead to promotion.

A skill scan for an Administrative Assistant:

Knowledge skills required	Know/can do	Know/but with help	Have to learn about	Target date
How to key in business letters	✔			
How to organise meetings		Yes, with help	Must speak with boss to clarify this task	Next week (Friday)
How to file the minutes of meetings	✔			
How to send emails			Not used the company email yet. Must ask to be shown.	I am being trained next month

ON-THE-JOB TRAINING

Training can be classified as either **'on-the-job'** or **'off-the-job'**. 'On-the-job' training involves the employees receiving their training at the place of work. Examples of this are as follows:

Work shadowing
Work shadowing involves a new member of staff following an experienced member of staff for a specified period of time so they can observe them at work and understand how they do their job.

Apprenticeships
Apprenticeships usually involve on-the-job training, where the apprentice works and trains in the workplace for part of the week as well as off-the-job training.

'Sitting next to Nellie'
This method involves an experienced employee demonstrating a task to a trainee, who then undertakes the task. The experienced employee supports the trainee until they are totally competent at the task.

Coaching
With **coaching**, a trainer takes a trainee through a task, step-by-step. The trainer is always on hand to support and coach the trainee. The idea is that the 'coach' will pass on their skills and knowledge to the trainee by being a mentor.

Job Rotation
Job rotation is where a trainee learns tasks in different departments/jobs. This is how supermarkets usually train employees, by rotating them round different departments such as checkout, clothing, home products, bakery and electrics.

OFF-THE-JOB TRAINING

'Off-the job' training involves the employees attending courses away from their workplace. Examples of this are as follows:

Courses at college and university
This involves employees attending courses away from their workplace, for example at colleges or universities.

Self-paced/distance learning
The employee is given resources such as a training manual and works on their own, usually at home.

Apprenticeships
Apprenticeships also usually involve off-the-job training, where the apprentice attends college for part of the week.

All the training courses that employees attend need to be evaluated to determine if they provide value for money for the business. HRM usually carries out this evaluation by asking the employee to complete a short questionnaire about the training course.

ONLINE

TASK 24: Visit www. brightredbooks.net/ N5BusMgmt and complete the task about staff training in well-known organisations.

ONLINE

PROGRESS CHECK 12: Visit www.brightredbooks.net/ N5BusMgmt and test your knowledge of staff training.

ONLINE TEST

How well have you learned this topic? Take the 'training' test at www.brightredbooks. net/N5BusMgmt

THINGS TO DO AND THINK ABOUT

The new teacher of English has been appointed to the English Department at your school. (Look back at online tasks 21 and 22 to remind yourself of this.) You now have to draw up an induction training programme to help them settle in.

Discuss with your teacher what this programme might include. Remember to ask about school policies on absence, health and safety training and how to carry out the role and day-to-day duties involved in the job. Word process this document and print it out.

TRAINING 2

APPRAISAL

This is a report on how well an employee is progressing. It is usually carried out at regular intervals (at least once a year) by the employee's line manager. The process usually requires both parties to fill in an appraisal form, and this is then followed up with a formal interview.

It is important that the employee does not feel that they are on trial, otherwise an element of distrust and resentment will arise.

The **appraisal** can highlight training needs or, on the other hand, that an employee is ready for promotion within the organisation. A successful appraisal could even lead to an employee receiving a bonus or moving up the pay scale.

A formal appraisal system should be used to:

- evaluate the performance of employees
- identify strengths and weaknesses of individual employees
- identify employees who might be ready for promotion
- assess the effectiveness of the recruitment and selection process – are the best people being employed?
- increase the motivation of employees
- improve communications between management and staff
- identify training needs
- award salary increases
- set future performance targets for individual employees.

Advantages of an appraisal system

Appraisals should encourage regular discussions between employers and employees, so they both have the opportunity to discuss any issues or concerns. This improves communication and working relationships within the business. By giving positive feedback to employees about their strengths and identifying their training needs, the business shows that it is interested in them. Employees will consequently feel more valued and committed to their job and will work harder.

Disadvantages of an appraisal system

Sometimes employees feel very threatened by an appraisal process. They could feel that the person appraising them isn't fair or doesn't like them, and so they won't feel confident about discussing issues.

Some staff are worried that the appraisal system is the management's way of 'getting rid' of them.

Employees might also lack confidence in speaking out at an appraisal meeting and, as a result, don't say how they **really** feel.

COSTS OF TRAINING

The costs of training are as follows:

Financial costs	These will include the cost of the course itself, plus travel and other expenses such as overnight accommodation. It can therefore become very expensive when a large number of employees have to attend the course.
Specialist training staff	If the organisation employs/hires specialist trainers to run a training and development course, the organisation will have to pay their salaries and provide accommodation for them.
Loss of output	When people are away from their job – for example, to attend a training or development activity – they will not be doing any work. In some cases, the organisation might therefore have to employ other workers on a temporary basis to fill in for these employees.

BENEFITS OF TRAINING

The benefits of training are as follows:

More flexible and adaptable employees	Employees who possess a wide range of skills are more flexible and adaptable, and so should find it easier to undertake a range of different roles within the business.
Easier to introduce and manage change	When an organisation invests in training and developing their staff, the organisation should find it much easier to introduce change with much less opposition from employees.
Employees have up-to-date skills	The changing environment faced by many organisations means that workers of all kinds must regularly update and improve their skills – for example, in ICT.
Increased employee satisfaction	Training and development can help the workforce to become more motivated, because they will have the chance to make use of a wider range of skills.
Employees are better prepared for promotion	Trained and highly skilled workers are better prepared to undertake promoted posts.
Improved motivation and productivity	An organisation with a satisfied, well-trained and well-motivated workforce tends to perform more effectively than one where this is not the case.
Improved image and reputation	A good training and development programme can help an organisation to attract new members of staff. Also, it can help the business to gain a good reputation with customers, especially where staff have undergone training in customer service.

ONLINE

PROGRESS CHECK 13: Visit www.brightredbooks.net/ N5BusMgmt and test your knowledge of staff training.

ONLINE TEST

How well have you learned this topic? Take the 'Staff training' test at www. brightredbooks.net/ N5BusMgmt

THINGS TO DO AND THINK ABOUT

Choose a partner. You are going to role-play an appraisal interview. The context is as follows. You both work for an electrical goods outlet. One person has to play the employee, the other the appraiser. The employee is lacking in confidence, and has been struggling to meet their sales targets and the appraiser wants to address this and find a way forward. When you have finished, swap around - the appraiser becomes the employee, and the employee the appraiser. Discuss what you have learned.

RETAINING AND MOTIVATING STAFF 1

EXTENSION

The depth of information on motivating and retaining staff in this section is extension material which will be useful if you go on to study for Higher Business Management.

WHY IT IS IMPORTANT TO RETAIN AND MOTIVATE STAFF

Having a happy and motivated workforce is vital for most business organisations, because it tends to result in:

- higher rates of productivity or output
- better quality output
- lower rates of absenteeism
- lower rates of labour turnover (staff leaving the organisation).

When an organisation invests time and money recruiting and training staff, it is important that these employees stay with the business for as long as possible. Where there are high levels of staff turnover, the business could be losing highly trained staff to business competitors, and it will also have to spend more time and money recruiting and training replacement employees.

There are also very specific reasons why it is important for a business to retain staff.

Company health

If the workforce is stable, management can invest its energy in moving the company forward. Management are not distracted by the need to continually hire new (replacement) employees, so they can concentrate on other areas like marketing new products, finding new suppliers and researching new methods of production.

Workers

With a stable workforce, employees are surrounded by co-workers who know their jobs, know each other, and know what they're all striving to do together as a company. They're able to focus on productivity and customer satisfaction instead of continually showing new employees how to do their jobs.

Customers

If a business has an unstable workforce, customers might have a nagging feeling that inadequate workers will miss critical deliveries or provide a product/service that is not up to standard. If customers don't have confidence in their suppliers, they'll buy from another business.

Investors

Increasingly, 'savvy' investors monitor workforce stability in companies where they invest – or are considering investing. Stability is vital to them. Continually pumping resources into recruitment, training, and rebuilding the workforce is not the best use of shareholders' money.

The industry

Recruiting new workers into an industry is essential for the continued health of all businesses in the industry. Well-trained/educated workers look for career paths that show promise of personal and professional opportunity, with good working conditions and rewards. Constant instability across the industry workforce could send out loud signals that this career path is not a wise decision and qualified workers will seek employment in other industries. This could lead to a skills shortage across the entire industry.

MAIN FACTORS AFFECTING MOTIVATION OF STAFF

The main factors that affect the motivation of staff are as follows:

- pay levels
- job security
- promotional prospects
- being given responsibilities
- working conditions
- fringe benefits like company cars and private health care
- participation in decision-making
- working as part of a team and being valued by team members.

FINANCIAL METHODS OF MOTIVATING AND RETAINING STAFF

There are many different payment methods that a business can use to motivate its workforce. The main methods are:

Time-rate or 'flat rate' schemes

This payment method involves employees receiving a basic rate of pay per time period that they work – for example, £5 per hour, £50 per day, £400 per week. The pay is not related to output or productivity as there is no incentive for employees to increase output.

Piece-rate schemes

This payment method involves employees receiving a specific amount of money for every unit (or 'piece') that they produce. Their pay is, therefore, directly linked to their productivity level. Employees are encouraged to increase output but quality could be sacrificed.

Commission

This is a common method of payment for sales staff – for example, in insurance and double-glazing. Employees receive a very small percentage (say 0.5 per cent) of the value of the goods/service that they manage to sell in a period of time. This encourages sales staff to sell more of the business's products which can increase their market share.

Profit sharing

This involves each employee receiving a share of the profit of the business each year. It aims to increase the levels of effort, motivation and productivity of each employee, since they stand to gain a share of any profit made.

Performance-related pay (PRP)

With this method, an individual who has achieved a certain number of targets over the past year will be given a pay rise. This is common with managerial and professional workers.

 DON'T FORGET

If a workforce is demotivated, it means that people are more likely to leave. Where there are high levels of staff turnover, the business could be losing highly trained staff to business competitors, and it will also have to spend more time and money recruiting and training replacement employees.

 CASE STUDY

Head to p90 and check out case study 9, on Green's.

 ONLINE TEST

How well have you learned this topic? Take the 'Retaining and motivating staff' test at www.brightredbooks.net/N5BusMgmt

 ## THINGS TO DO AND THINK ABOUT

Ask your teacher for information about how your school retains and motivates teaching and non-teaching staff. What are the main factors motivating staff at your school?

RETAINING AND MOTIVATING STAFF 2

NON-FINANCIAL METHODS OF MOTIVATING AND RETAINING STAFF

There are many non-financial methods that different managers use to motivate and retain their workforce. These include:

Delegation

This occurs when managers pass a degree of authority down the hierarchy to workers on the 'shop floor'. This allows workers to make decisions for themselves and shows that managers respect and trust them. Employees feel more valued and are likely to work harder.

Job rotation

This involves giving employees the opportunity to perform a variety of different tasks within their job to make it more interesting and to avoid repetition. This leads to higher levels of motivation. Supermarkets also rotate staff round different areas of work (clothing, fruit and vegetables, bakery and fresh meats) to offer more challenge, interest and opportunity.

Worker participation

This refers to the participation of workers in the decision-making process, where they are asked for their ideas and suggestions. Workers feel more valued by the organisation.

Team-working

Employees work in teams, so that each individual worker feels a sense of commitment and responsibility towards the team. As a result, the team is likely to be more successful in achieving targets. Team achievement is likely to motivate workers.

Job enlargement

This involves increasing the number of tasks that are involved in performing a particular job. The aim is to make the job more challenging and less repetitive to motivate employees and make them more multi-skilled.

Fringe Benefits

These are benefits in addition to wages or salary given to the employee by the employer. Examples include:
- gym membership
- health insurance
- company car
- employee discounts
- childcare assistance
- cafeteria vouchers.

Flexible working practices

In an attempt to retain and motivate staff, employers can offer a range of flexible working practices:

- **Part-time working** – this offers employees the opportunity to work less than the standard 35 hours per week.

- **Homeworking** – employees are given the opportunity to work from home, using information technology to communicate with the business. The business does not need to purchase or rent large premises when a number of employees work from home.

contd

- **Teleworking** – employees can work away from the office, using technology (iPhones, and e-mail) to communicate with the business.

- **Flexi-time** – offers employees greater flexibility in their start and finish times so long as they are at work during the 'core time' specified by the employer. Employees can attend personal appointments, for example doctors appointments, in their own time and so working hours are not lost attending personal appointments.

- **Job share** – two people share a full-time job. One employee might work the first half of the week and the other employee the second half of the week. Effective and highly trained employees who wish to reduce working hours can be retained by the business.

MOTIVATION PROBLEMS AND HOW BUSINESSES SOLVE THEM

Poor motivation in the workforce usually results in the following problems:

- high rates of absenteeism
- high level of staff turnover (staff leaving)
- poor timekeeping
- unnecessary waste and spoiled output
- low quality output
- disciplinary problems and grievances.

When motivation is low and employees are unhappy with their terms and conditions or work, they might take the following types of industrial action:

- **work to rule** – employees will only undertake the duties outlined in their contract of employment. All 'goodwill' is withdrawn. Working to rule can lead to poor working relationships between employees and employers.

- **go slow** – workers work slower than normal to deliberately reduce output. This can lead to orders not being fulfilled, and so a reduction in customer satisfaction.

- **strike** – employees refuse to enter the business's premises. They may demonstrate outside the business to highlight their concerns. This means that production stops, customers could go elsewhere and the business could develop a reputation of being unreliable.

If a business has a poor level of motivation and is experiencing these problems, management should do the following:

- build a strong team spirit
- review pay levels to ensure employees are being paid fairly
- design more challenging jobs for employees
- give praise and recognition to employees for their efforts and achievements.

ONLINE

PROGRESS CHECK 14: Visit www.brightredbooks.net/N5BusMgmt and test your knowledge of retaining and motivating staff.

ONLINE TEST

How well have you learned this topic? Take the 'Retaining and motivating staff' test at www.brightredbooks.net/N5BusMgmt

THINGS TO DO AND THINK ABOUT

1 Myres and Johnstone plc are concerned about the high turnover of staff. Outline some flexible working practices that Myres and Johnstone plc could offer their employees in order to retain their services for longer.

2 Employees at Myres and Johnstone plc are unhappy with their current terms and conditions of employment. Outline two types of industrial action that employees at Myres and Johnstone plc could decide to take.

3 Describe two effects that the industrial action outlined in question 2 above could have on Myres and Johnstone plc.

4 Jane Sturrock currently works full-time at Myres and Johnstne plc as a Receptionist. Jane wants to have a better work-life balance. Suggest a flexible working practice that could be offered to Jane.

EMPLOYMENT LEGISLATION

HUMAN RESOURCES AND EMPLOYMENT LEGISLATION

The Human Resources Department must make sure that all of the organisation's policies and procedures are in line with current employment legislation. **Employment legislation** is constantly changing and being updated and so the Human Resources Department must ensure that all managers are aware of these laws and any changes to them. There could be severe legal consequences if they don't. There are three main pieces of legislation:

- **Health and Safety at Work Act 1974**
- **Data Protection Act 1998**
- **Freedom of Information (Scotland) Act 2002**

DON'T FORGET

All organisations need to ensure that their policies and procedures are in line with current employment legislation. If they don't keep up to date with these laws, there could be severe legal consequences.

Health and Safety at Work Act 1974

Anyone entering these premises must comply with regulations covered by the above act.

ONLINE

TASK 25: Visit www. brightredbooks.net/ N5BusMgmt and design a poster highlighting the aims of the HASAWA.

Health and Safety at Work Act 1974 (HASAWA)

This Act applies to all workplaces and the people working there. It states that **employees *and* employers** have responsibilities. It is an umbrella act which covers all premises and everyone at work. Under the umbrella are a variety of other acts and regulations that cover specific subjects such as first aid, fire and visual display units (VDUs).

Responsibilities of employers	Responsibilities of employees
Provide and maintain a suitable working environment.	Take reasonable care for their own safety and the safety of others.
Provide staff with training and safety information.	Cooperate with employer on health and safety matters.
Provide staff with protective clothing/equipment if needed.	Do not misuse or tamper or interfere with equipment – for example, fire extinguishers.
Provide a Health and Safety Policy.	

The HASAWA also covers basic health, safety and welfare such as heating, lighting, ventilation, space and toilet facilities

Data Protection Act 1998

This law was created in 1984 to protect computer-based information but paper-based information was added in 1998.

All **data users** must register with the Data Protection Registrar so that they can monitor:
- the nature of the data (**what**)
- the reason for the data being kept (**why**)
- the method used to collect the data (**how**)
- the parties/people data will be passed on to (**who**).

contd

If an organisation is dealing with personal data – information about people such as their age, address or occupation – they must keep to the principles of good practice. **The principles of good practice** state that personal data must:

- be obtained fairly and lawfully
- be used for the registered purpose only
- not be disclosed for any other reason than is given to the Registrar
- be relevant, adequate and not excessive for the purpose
- be accurate and kept up to date
- not be kept for longer than is needed
- be available to the data subject and be changed if it is not accurate
- be secure – there must be steps taken to keep it safe from unauthorised access or from being lost.

If an organisation goes against these principles or fails to register with the Registrar, they could be prosecuted and face fines of up to £5000. The information might be taken away from them. Subjects who feel that the data stored about them is not accurate can complain or request compensation for distress caused.

Freedom of Information (Scotland) Act 2002

This Act has made it possible for members of the public to request information that is held about them from a public body – for example, the National Health Service (NHS). People must now be told whether the public body holds information about them and they have the right to see that information within 20 days from the date it was requested. Under this Act, however, information can be withheld if it affects national security or if it would mean breaching the Data Protection Act 1998.

Equality Act 2010

The Equality Act 2010 covers individuals at work and when they use services such as shops, hotels, gyms, hospitals and other free services. The characteristics that are protected by the Equality Act 2010 are: age, disability, gender, marriage or civil partnership, preganacy or maternity, race, religion or blief, sex and sexual orientation.

ONLINE

TASK 26: Visitwww. brightredbooks.net/ N5BusMgmt and complete the task about other important employment legislation.

ONLINE

PROGRESS CHECK 15: Visit www.brightredbooks.net/ N5BusMgmt and test your knowledge of employment legislation.

ONLINE TEST

How well have you learned this topic? Take the 'Employment legislation' test at www.brightredbooks.net/ N5BusMgmt

THINGS TO DO AND THINK ABOUT

There are a number of other key employment laws that organisations need to know about and keep up to date with. These are as follows:

- **Sex Discrimination Act 1975**
- **Equal Pay Act 1970**
- **Race Relations Act 1976**
- **Disability Discrimination Act 1995**
- **Display Screen Equipment Act – Health and Safety at Work Act 1992**
- **Control of Substances Hazardous to Health Regulations Act**

You will already be familiar with the basic purpose of these Acts if you have completed task 26 online. You're now going to look at one of these Acts in more detail.

Select one of the Acts listed below:

- **Sex Discrimination Act 1975**
- **Disability Discrimination Act 1995**
- **Race Relations Act 1976**

Use the internet to research the Act you have selected. For example, you could find out the aims of the Act and the consequences for organisations who fail to adhere to it.

Prepare a PowerPoint presentation to present your research to the class.

Ensure your name is clearly displayed on your PowerPoint presentation and print one copy.

SOURCES OF FINANCE 1

OVERVIEW

Finance is important to **every** organisation – from sole traders to large public limited companies – because all organisations have to deal with money. However, different types of organisations have different financial objectives.

- Sole traders and partnerships need to earn sufficient profit to justify the risk of being in business. If a sole trader or partners can earn more by working for someone else, then employment is probably the less risky option.

- The financial objective of all companies in the private sector is to earn profit. Indeed, shareholders and other investors will expect a healthy profit each year and could actually vote to remove a board of directors when this is not achieved.

- The financial objective of charities and voluntary sector organisations is to raise as many donations/funds as possible. They must also use their funds as effectively as possible to further their cause or to help as many people in need as possible.

- Public funded organisations will aim to manage their spending in line with the limited budget that they have been allocated from central or local government.

Good financial management is crucial to ensure the success of any organisation. For example, every organisation must make sure that it has:

- enough money to pay the wages and salaries of its employees

- a good grasp on how much it is spending to ensure efficiency – organisations that have high costs are often unsuccessful

- sufficient money to pay its bills for supplies of raw materials, stock from suppliers, electricity, advertising and insurance etc.

- sufficient money to invest in developing new products and services, or it may be overtaken by competitors

- identified and organised additional sources of funds should it require access to these in the future.

WHY DOES A BUSINESS NEED FINANCE?

Businesses need finance for a number of reasons.

Capital expenditure

To set up a business, money (or capital) is required to finance aspects such as the purchase of premises, machinery, fixtures and fittings and equipment.

Day-to-day business activities

Money is also needed to finance day-to-day business activities: for example, purchasing stock from suppliers, paying wages to employees and paying business expenses such as heat and light, insurance and advertising costs.

contd

Expansion

Most businesses start small and grow. A business can only expand if it has access to the necessary finance.

Research into new products and services

If a business wants to be a market leader and stay ahead of the competition, it will need to finance the research, development and marketing of new products and services.

PESTEC

A business needs finance to deal with external factors (PESTEC). When the economy is in recession, a business might temporarily require access to additional finance to cope with a fall in normal sales levels.

FACTORS AFFECTING SOURCES OF FINANCE

So finance is essential at all stages in the life of a business, whether it is a relatively inexperienced entrepreneur just starting up or a long-standing business with a successful history and a proven track record.

There are a range of sources of finance available to a business. However, access to these will depend on a number of factors:

- **What is the finance for?** Starting a new business or expanding a successful existing business?

- **How much finance is required?** Smaller amounts of money might be more readily available. Lenders and/or investors might be more reluctant to provide larger amounts of money.

- **Does the money need to be paid back and, if so, when?** Some sources of finance can be paid back over many years. Other sources will require fairly quick repayment – for example, within one month or within one year. When money has to be repaid, it is more than likely that interest will also have to be paid.

- **How big is the organisation?** Large, established organisations with a good credit history are usually in a favourable position to obtain finance from lenders/investors. They also tend to have assets such as expensive machinery or equipment that they can offer lenders/investors as security, should they fail to repay. However, new or smaller organisations are less likely to have the means to survive the impact of PESTEC so they are more of a risk and, therefore, less attractive to lenders/investors.

- **How well-known and established is the business?** An established, reputable business with a proven track record will probably be able to secure finance more easily than a relatively new, inexperienced and unknown business with an unknown credit history.

ONLINE

TASK 27: Visit www. brightredbooks.net/ N5BusMgmt and discuss the questions on sources of finance.

ONLINE TEST

How well have you learned this topic? Take the 'Sources of finance' test at www.brightredbooks.net/ N5BusMgmt

THINGS TO DO AND THINK ABOUT

You are a young entrepreneur, and you want to start up a business selling fair trade gifts in a village popular with tourists. Which factors will you have to think about before you apply for sources of finance? Discuss this in a group and write your notes on a sheet of paper or in your workbook.

SOURCES OF FINANCE 2

SHORT-TERM SOURCES OF FINANCE

Short-term sources of finance deal with short-term cash flow problems – for example, from a three to six month period up to a maximum of a year.

Source of finance	Advantages	Disadvantages
Bank overdraft	An overdraft allows the business to overdraw its bank account – to spend more money than it has, up to an agreed amount. The business can, therefore, continue to pay business expenses despite having no money in the bank account.	Banks charge high rates of interest on overdrawn amounts, so this can be expensive if used for a long period of time. Also, banks can withdraw the overdraft facility at any time.
Trade credit	Trade credit allows a business to buy goods and pay for them at a later date. This gives the business time to sell stock at a higher price and earn a profit before the bill from the supplier has to be paid.	Cash discount for prompt payment to suppliers is likely to be lost. If payment is not made within the agreed credit period, suppliers will be reluctant to offer credit to the business in the future.
Factoring	Most businesses offer credit facilities to their customers. If customers are late with their payment or don't pay at all, the business can use a factoring service. The factor buys the customer's debt for a **reduced amount** and then takes responsibility for collecting (chasing up) the amount owed from customers. This provides the business with the cash it needs without the hassle of trying to collect the money from customers.	The business doesn't receive the full amount owed by its customers so, overall, there is less money 'flowing in' to the business. Factors are only likely to offer their services when there are large amounts of debts owed by the business's customers.
Grant	This is money given to a business by central or local government, the EU or from the Prince's Trust for things such as the purchase of new machinery or training of staff. It is often used to persuade businesses to locate in areas of high unemployment. It doesn't have to be paid back.	Grants can be complicated to apply for and the business often needs to meet many conditions before they are awarded the grant. Grants are usually one-off payments that are not repeated.
Retained profits	An established business will usually 'hold' or retain profit from previous years in the business. Retained profits can be used to buy more stock or to take advantage of bulk buying, which should increase future profits.	When a business has to continually use retained profits to solve short-term cash flow problems, it is often unable to grow and expand at the speed it would like to.

MEDIUM-TERM SOURCES OF FINANCE

Medium-term sources of finance are normally agreed over a one to five year time period.

Source of finance	Advantages	Disadvantages
Bank loan	A bank loan is usually granted for a fixed amount, and has to be paid back in fixed monthly instalments over a fixed period of time – for example, five years. The business can budget for the monthly repayments and is able to purchase essential machinery or equipment straightaway.	Interest has to be paid in addition to the loan itself. New and relatively small businesses might find it difficult to convince lenders to give them a loan.

contd

Leasing	A business can 'rent' vehicles or other equipment from a leasing company, so it doesn't have to use its limited financial resources to purchase expensive assets. The leasing company is responsible for the maintenance and upgrading of the equipment.	The business will never actually own the asset. Renting costs can soon mount up to the extent that it might actually be cheaper to purchase the asset in the first place.
Hire purchase	Hire purchase allows a business to buy an asset, such as a delivery van, and pay it back over a fixed period of time – for example, 36 months. An initial deposit is required, followed by monthly payments. This allows a business to purchase expensive equipment with only an initial deposit.	The business does not legally own the asset until the last hire purchase payment has been made. If interest rates are high, then this can be an expensive form of borrowing.

LONG-TERM SOURCES OF FINANCE

Long-term sources of finance are normally agreed over a five- to 20-year time period, and are often used to expand the business.

Source of finance	Advantages	Disadvantages
Owner's personal finance	This includes using personal savings or borrowing money from family and friends who are willing to support the business. The main advantage is that borrowing is reduced and the owner(s) maintain control of the business.	All of these savings and this money could be invested in a business that does not succeed. It's a risk for those involved. Owners could lose all their capital if they have unlimited liability.
Share issue	This source of finance is available to public limited companies and can be a good method of raising large amounts of capital. People who buy shares (shareholders) will receive an annual dividend in return for their investment. The money does not have to be repaid.	Shareholders become part owners of the business. The advertising and legal aspects of this can be very expensive and time consuming.
Debenture	This is a source of finance used by public limited companies. Debentures are a type of long-term loan. Lenders receive a fixed rate of interest each year. After 20 to 25 years the business can repay the loan. Large amounts of money can be raised. Investors sometimes give debentures (loans) for projects that the banks have not been prepared to support.	Debenture interest must be paid each year, even if the business makes a loss. If the business fails, debenture holders have the right to sell assets (for example, machinery, equipment and motor vehicles) to retrieve the money they lent the business.
Mortgage	A common method of financing the purchase of land and premises is to take a mortgage from a bank, where a long-term loan is secured against the title deeds for the land or buildings of a property. The bank or other mortgage provider retains ownership of the land or premises until the entire mortgage has been repaid. The business is generally given a long period (20–25 years) to repay the mortgage.	If the borrower doesn't meet the monthly mortgage repayments, the lender can claim ownership of the property and sell it to retrieve the money they lent the business. Interest is charged for the duration of the mortgage in addition to the actual mortgage repayments. This can be very expensive.

ONLINE

TASK 28: Visit www. brightredbooks.net/ N5BusMgmt and try the task on sources of finance.

ONLINE

PROGRESS CHECK 16: Visit www.brightredbooks.net/ N5BusMgmt and test your knowledge of sources of finance.

ONLINE TEST

How well have you learned this topic? Take the 'Sources of finance' test at www.brightredbooks.net/ N5BusMgmt

THINGS TO DO AND THINK ABOUT

Look at your notes from the previous section. You want to open a fair trade shop in a village popular with tourists. In the same group, discuss which sources of finance you might consider to get your business started.

CASH BUDGETING 1

OVERVIEW

Businesses generate cash by buying and selling goods and/or services. Good financial management and efficient cash budgeting are crucial to the success of every organisation. Whether it's a sole trader or a huge public limited company, each organisation needs to ensure that it has:

- enough money to pay the wages and salaries of its employees

- monitored how much it is spending to ensure that it is efficient – organisations that have high costs are often unsuccessful

- enough money to pay its bills – for example, for supplies of raw materials, stock from suppliers, electricity, advertising and insurance

- enough money to invest in developing new products and services – or it could be overtaken by its competitors

- identified and organised additional sources of funds in case it needs these in the future.

WHY CASH FLOW ISSUES OCCUR

Cash flow problems can arise even if the firm is successful and is selling a lot of its goods. If goods are being sold on **credit**, customers **do not pay** for their goods straight away. Indeed, some customers might take longer than expected to pay and some might not even pay at all (as they themselves could be having financial difficulties). This situation can lead to cash flow problems because the company has to pay for its stock and for expenses, such as heat, light, petrol, rent and wages, before it gets money in from its customers. Effectively, a cash flow issue is when a business has insufficient cash to cover its day to day expenditure.

HOW CASH FLOW ISSUES CAN BE RESOLVED

A business can resolve its cash flow issues by taking one or more of the following courses of action:

Raising additional capital

Re-investing profits in the business, issuing shares to the public and injecting more personal finance into the business will create a healthy cash inflow.

Taking out loans

Organising a loan from a bank – or in the case of sole traders from family or friends – will create a cash inflow. However, repayments with interest will represent a cash outflow.

Tight credit control

The business should ensure that it collects money owed by customers as quickly as possible. This will improve the inflow of cash to the business.

Delay making payments

The business should take longer to pay bills for business expenses and bills from the suppliers of stock. By doing this, the organisation will reduce the outflow of cash until cash has been received from customers.

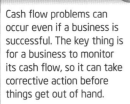

DON'T FORGET

Cash flow problems can occur even if a business is successful. The key thing is for a business to monitor its cash flow, so it can take corrective action before things get out of hand.

contd

Efficient stock control

The business should ensure that cash is not tied up in large amounts of stock. This will ensure that cash outflow is kept at a sensible level.

Spreading purchase costs

The business can avoid making large one-off payments for the purchase of equipment and machinery. Hire purchase or leasing allows the cost to be spread over several months.

WHAT IS A CASH BUDGET?

A **cash budget** is a plan of how much money you have and how you will spend it.

The accountant and the finance department are responsible for managing the money/cash within a business. A cash budget shows the money that comes in and goes out of the business during the year. Preparing a cash budget should mean that:

- the business finances are better controlled and money is spent wisely
- the business can see where problems in its cash flow will arise. For example, if there is likely to be a shortage of cash one month, then an overdraft can be arranged in advance. If the cash shortage will last for some time, a loan can be arranged to cover it
- decisions can be taken about the best time to make a big outlay of cash – for example, to purchase machinery or equipment.

A cash budget is sometimes prepared in advance, but unforeseen events mean that it doesn't always go completely to plan, and so it has to be adjusted or revised.

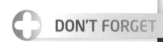
DON'T FORGET

A cash budget is a plan of how much money a business has, and how the business will spend it.

ONLINE TEST

How well have you learned this topic? Take the 'Cash budgeting' test at www.brightredbooks.net/N5BusMgmt.

THINGS TO DO AND THINK ABOUT

Cash flow problems can occur if customers take longer than expected to pay, or don't pay at all. Think of two other situations that could cause cash flow problems in a business, and think about how you would solve them. Write your ideas down on A4 paper and discuss them with the class.

CASH BUDGETING 2

PRODUCING A CASH BUDGET

A cash budget begins with the opening balance. This is the amount of money expected to be available to the business at the start of the month.

The next step is to anticipate the money that is likely to be received for the month and add this to the opening balance.

After this, all the payments that the business expects to make during the month are taken away. This gives the closing balance, or the amount of money left at the end of the month. The closing balance for one month becomes the opening balance for the next month.

Here's an example of a cash budget for Jack Clark, who is a sole trader. The information applies to the first quarter of the year:

EXAMPLE:

Cash Budget for Jack Clark

	Jan	Feb	March	April
Opening Cash Balance	6000	−2200	−5400	−2850
Money in				
Cash Sales	600	600	650	700
Credit Sales	4000	4000	5400	5400
	10 600	2400	650	3250
Money out				
Purchases	2000	2000	2500	3000
Advertising	300	300	300	300
Wages	500	500	500	500
Rent	6000			
Fixtures and Fittings	4000			
Delivery Van		5000		
Electricity			200	
	12 800	7800	3500	3800
Closing Cash Balance	-2200	−5400	−2850	−550

Jack can now use the cash budget to plan ahead and to make decisions that will enable him to manage his cash flow and pay his bills. For example, Jack has decided that in February he wants to buy a new delivery van for the business.

The total cost will be £5000. By planning ahead and looking at his cash budget, Jack realises that he cannot afford it just now as he does not have enough cash to buy it. Therefore, to ensure his business does not get into cash flow problems, Jack could consider:

- arranging a bank loan to purchase the van: this would allow Jack to purchase the van straight away without having to 'fork' out a large amount of money in one month. The total cost of the van could be spread over a number of months. However, interest would have to be paid to the bank in addition to the repayments for the loan.

- leasing a van: Jack could simply rent a van from a leasing company. This way he gets his van but without having to 'fork' out large sums of money in any one month. Jack would simply make monthly rental payments.

The cash budget is, therefore, used to help with decision making in a business. A cash budget shows whether there is enough money for the business to do what it plans to do. More importantly, it can show whether a business needs to find cash from somewhere else.

ACTIVITY

Interpreting a cash budget, identifying problems and suggesting suitable solutions

Now that you have seen an example of a cash budget, you're going to prepare one of your own. Go through the following activity with your teacher, and then have a go at online tasks 29 and 30 on your own.

 THINGS TO DO AND THINK ABOUT

The following task requires you to prepare a cash budget for a sole trader's business. You can do this manually, by completing the grid below (using a calculator) or you can use a spreadsheet to complete each task.

R Jeeves starts his business with an opening balance of £1000 on 1 January.

He has also received a bank loan on 1 January for £10 000 from his local bank.

His plans for the first six months of trading are:

1   Payments to Cash and Carry for supplies – Jan £5500; Feb £7200; March £9700; April £10 500; May £9600; June £6900.

2   Receipts from customers – Jan £3900; Feb £5900; March £6000; April £7100; May £8400; June £15 500.

3   The bank loan will be repaid at £500 per month, plus £50 interest starting on 1 March.

4   Drawings per calendar month – £300.

5   You are required to draw up a cash budget for the six months, showing the opening and closing balance for each month. The first two months have been completed for you.

J Reeves: Cash Budget for January – June						
	Jan	**Feb**	**Mar**	**Apr**	**May**	**June**
	£	£	£	£	£	£
Opening balance	1000	9100				
Money in						
Receipts from customers	3900	5900				
Loan	10 000					
	14 900	5900				
Money out						
Payments to cash & carry	5500	7200				
Loan repayment					.	
Loan interest						
Drawings	300	300				
	5800	7500				
Closing balance	9100	7500				

During which months does J Reeves experience cash flow problems?

Suggest an appropriate source of finance that he could access to help him during these months.

Now that you have prepared this cash budget, try two more.

 ONLINE

TASK 29: visit www.brightredbooks.net/N5BusMgmt and prepare a cash budget for N Norris.

ONLINE

TASK 30: visit www.brightredbooks.net/N5BusMgmt and prepare a cash budget for J Clarke.

 ONLINE TEST

How well have you learned this topic? Take the 'Cash budgeting' test at www.brightredbooks.net/N5BusMgmt

BREAK-EVEN 1

What products should I make or sell?

How many products should I make or sell?

How much profit will I earn, if any, from selling a product?

PURPOSE OF BREAK-EVEN ANALYSIS

Break-even analysis is a useful tool for any profit-making business. It can help a business to answer some very important questions:

Is producing or selling a certain product going to be profitable?

If no profit is being made from making/selling a product, there is no point in the business continuing to make/sell that product. It would be more sensible to put time and resources into making a product that **is** profitable.

How many units of a product would have to be sold before any profit is made?

A business can only produce/sell a certain product, for example motorcars, if it can do so on a very large scale. Making or selling only a small quantity could prove to be very costly and unprofitable.

What will the profit be at various levels of output?

A business will wish to forecast and plan for the future. As such, it will require an indication of profit at various levels of output/sales.

All businesses need to cover their costs. Costs are the payments made for materials, wages, expenses, rates, insurance, etc. Some costs are fixed and some costs are variable.

FIXED COSTS

These are costs such as rent, insurance and loan interest that are fixed and **do not change** no matter how many units are produced or sold. Fixed costs are the same for 2000 units as they are for 10 000 units. These costs still have to be paid, even if there is no output.

VARIABLE COSTS

These are costs such as raw materials and electricity that **do change** according to how many units are produced or sold. If there is no output, then variable costs will be nil.

TOTAL COSTS

Total costs are simply **fixed costs** and **variable costs** added together.

↓

$$TC = FC + VC$$

A business must pay **all its costs** before it can make a profit. As **total costs** include some of the **variable costs**, then total costs will also change with any changes in output/sales. For example, if output/sales rise then so will total costs. If output/sales fall, then total costs will also fall.

CALCULATING PROFIT AND LOSS AND BREAK-EVEN

We're now going to look at how to calculate the level of output at which a business will make a profit or loss, and the level of output at which it will break-even. The level of production where total costs = total revenue – that is, when no profit or loss is made – is known as the **break-even point**.

contd

EXAMPLE 1

A business has the following costs:

fixed costs	£12 000
variable costs	£18 000
total costs	£30 000 (£12 000 + £18 000)

If the business sells these goods for less than £30 000, they will make a **loss**.

If they sell the goods for exactly £30 000, they will **break even**.

If the business sells the goods for more than £30 000, they will make a **profit**.

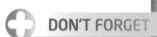

DON'T FORGET

The **break-even point** is where total costs and total income (revenue) are the same. At this point the business has not made any profit or loss.

EXAMPLE 2

Jim Bannerman makes and sells cupcakes.

He has **fixed costs** of £600 per annum.

The **variable costs** of making each cupcake include:

materials – 15p per unit
electricity – 60p per unit } 75p

Jim Bannerman **sells** each unit of output (cupcake) for £1 each.

Your teacher will help you to calculate the profit or loss at each of the various levels of output shown on the table below. The first one has been done for you.

Output	Sales revenue	Fixed costs	Variable costs	Total costs	Profit/loss
	Output × £1		Output × 75p	FC+VC	SR–TC
0	£0	£600	£0	£600	£600 Loss
400	£400	£600	£300	£900	£500 Loss
800					
1200					
1600					
2000					
2400					
2800					
3200					

Questions

At what level of output does Jim Bannerman not make a profit or a loss?

What is this level of output called?

At what level of output does the business first make a profit?

What costs does the business incur below the break-even point – at the point when it is making an output of 2000 units?

ONLINE TEST

How well have you learned this topic? Take the 'Break-even' test at www.brightredbooks.net/N5BusMgmt

THINGS TO DO AND THINK ABOUT

You've already calculated the profit, loss and break-even point of Jim Bannerman's cupcake business with your teacher. Now try this next activity on your own.

The following figures have been supplied by A Gardiner, who is considering making plant pots. He is particularly concerned to know how many he must make before the product becomes profitable.

fixed costs	£1000
variable costs per pot	£3
selling price per pot	£8

Complete the table below using the information above. The first row has been completed for you.

At what level of output does A Gardiner break-even?

Units of output	Fixed costs	Variable costs	Total costs	Sales revenue	Profit/(loss)
	FC	VC	FC+VC		
0	£1000	–	£1000	–	£1000 (loss)
100					
200					
300					
400					
500					

BREAK-EVEN 2

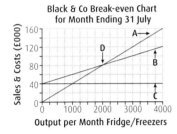

Black & Co Break-even Chart for Month Ending 31 July

Output per Month Fridge/Freezers

PRODUCING AND INTERPRETING BREAK-EVEN CHARTS

The break-even point (BEP) is calculated so that the firm can forecast the level of profit or the level of loss at a given number of items being produced. It also helps a business to decide the selling price of a product and to understand the effect that changing the selling price will have.

The break-even point can be shown in the form of a chart. There are three lines on each break-even chart. In this example – the Black and Co break-even chart for month ending 31 July – the lines are labelled A, B and C and the break-even point is labelled D.

A	This represents the total revenue (income received by the business) and always starts at 0 because if you sell nothing, you earn no revenue. As sales increase then so does total revenue.
B	This represents the total cost at each level of production or output. (The total cost equals fixed costs and variable costs added together.) Therefore, because total cost includes variable costs, total costs will increase or decrease with output.
C	This represents the fixed costs that must be paid, even if no products are sold. Fixed costs remain the same no matter the level of output and that's why it is shown as a straight line.
D	This is the break-even point – the point at which total costs and total revenue are the same and cross on the chart. At the break-even point no profit or loss is made.

The area of profit or loss at any level of output can be measured between the sales revenue line and total cost line:

- The area of **profit** in the Black and Co chart is the area to the **right** of point D.

- The area of **loss** in the Black and Co chart is the area to the **left** of the point D.

THE ADVANTAGES OF USING BREAK-EVEN ANALYSIS

A business can use break-even analysis to:

- calculate the break-even point in terms of units or sales revenue for each product it makes/sells

- estimate the profit or loss that will result at any given level of output or sales of a product

- find the level of output or number of sales that must be made to achieve the profit the business wants to earn.

THE DISADVANTAGES OF BREAK-EVEN ANALYSIS

- Break-even analysis assumes that there is only one product – most businesses produce/sell a range of products. Relying on one product would be very risky.

- The selling price remains the same for long periods of time. Selling price can change frequently (up or down) due to factors outwith the business's control. This can make break-even facts unreliable.

- Most costs can be classified as either fixed or variable, but there are some that can't. For example, telephone bills contain an element of both fixed and variable costs – the fixed line rental and the variable amount of phone calls made each month.

ONLINE

PROGRESS CHECK 17: Visit www.brightredbooks.net/ N5BusMgmt and test your knowledge of the break-even point.

THINGS TO DO AND THINK ABOUT

You have analysed an example of a break-even chart. Now have a go at drawing one up yourself. Read the information in the following two activities, and complete two different break-even charts – one for Janice Smith and one for J Kane.

Break-even chart for Janice Smith

Janice Smith decides to rent a stall at her local market for one year, with the purpose of selling ice cream. She has worked out her costs as follows:

Fixed costs

stall rental	£300
assistant's wages	£900
advertising	£10
electricity	£40
	£1250

Variable cost per ice-cream = 40p

Selling price per ice-cream = 50p

Copy and complete this break-even table.

Using the figures from the table you have completed, draw up a break-even chart on suitable graph paper to show the total costs, fixed costs and total sales line. You should also indicate the break-even point, the area of profit and the area of loss.

Now that you have prepared this break-even chart, try another one.

ONLINE TEST

How well have you learned this topic? Take the 'Break-even' test at www.brightredbooks.net/N5BusMgmt

Units Sold	Fixed costs	Variable costs	Total costs	Total sales	Profit or loss
0					
2500					
5000					
7500					
10000					
12500					
15000					
17500					
20000					

Break-even chart for J Kane

J Kane sells machinery to the farm industry. His fixed costs are £10000 and each machine costs him £400 (variable cost) to buy. He sells them for £600 each and is trying to work out his profit or loss at various levels of sales. He has worked out the following:

Units Sold	Fixed costs	Variable costs	Total costs	Sales revenue	Profit or loss
0	£10000	-		-	
10	£10000	£4000		£6000	
20	£10000	£8000		£12000	
30	£10000	£12000		£18000	
40	£10000	£16000		£24000	
50	£10000	£20000		£30000	
60	£10000	£24000		£36000	
70	£10000	£28000		£42000	
80	£10000	£32000		£48000	
90	£10000	£36000		£54000	
100	£10000	£40000		£60000	

1   Complete the total cost and profit/loss columns in the table.

2   Using the completed table, construct a break-even chart on a sheet of graph paper. You should plot total costs, fixed costs and sales revenue.

3   When you have completed your graph you should clearly show the break-even point, area of profit and area of loss.

Now that you have prepared these break-even charts, try two more online.

ONLINE

TASK 31: visit www.brightredbooks.net/N5BusMgmt and prepare a break-even chart.

ONLINE

TASK 32: visit www.brightredbooks.net/N5BusMgmt and prepare another break-even chart.

PROFIT STATEMENT

TRADING, PROFIT AND LOSS ACCOUNTS AND TECHNOLOGY

Profit is the difference between the money (revenue) received from the sale of a good or service and the cost of providing the good or service.

Everyone with money invested in a business – whether a sole trader, partner or a shareholder in a company – will be interested to know how much profit their business is making and how much they are likely to receive in return for the money they have invested.

This is why at the end each year a business prepares a Trading and Profit and Loss Account, which outlines how well the business has performed. The Trading and Profit and Loss Account is split into two sections:

The Trading Account

The **Trading Account** shows the profit or loss made from purchasing goods at one price (the cost price) and selling them at a higher price (the selling price). Therefore, the aim of the Trading Account is to calculate the **gross profit**.

The Profit and Loss Account

After the gross profit has been calculated in the Trading Account, the next step is to prepare the **Profit and Loss Account** where all the current year's expenses (for example, rent, wages, advertising and heat and light) are deducted from the gross profit. The resulting figure is called the **net profit**.

The figures for the Trading and Profit and Loss Account will have been taken from accurate records kept on every transaction the business makes from selling goods to paying the phone bill!

Look at the example below.

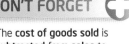

SMITH PLC		
TRADING, PROFIT AND LOSS ACCOUNT		
FOR YEAR ENDED 31 DECEMBER 2---		
	£	£
Sales		33,778
Less Cost of Sales		
Opening Stock	4,345	
Add Purchases	7,444	
	11,789	
Less Closing Stock	4,883	
COST OF SALES		6,906
Gross Profit		26,872
Less Expenses		
Rent	1,123	
Rates	555	
Telephone	366	
Salaries	9,077	
Light and Heat	1,743	12,864
Net Profit		14,008

Example Trading Profit and Loss Account

All businesses prepare a Trading and Profit and Loss Account at least once per year. However, public limited companies must also publish their Trading and Profit and Loss Account for shareholders, investors and members of the public to examine.

Technology

Most finance departments use spreadsheet software, such as Microsoft Excel, to help them to prepare cash budgets and Trading and Profit and Loss Accounts.

The user can enter formulae into the spreadsheet so that numbers can be added, subtracted, divided and multiplied to produce financial statements.

Graphs can also be created to display financial information more effectively. Financial information can also be edited relatively quickly and saved for future use.

HOW PROFITS ARE USED

- A **sole trader** gets to keep all the profits once tax has been paid on them. This is their reward for taking a risk and achieving success.
- In a **partnership**, the profits will be distributed amongst the partners in a ratio agreed by the partners when the business was set up.
- In a **public limited company**, the Board of Directors will decide what percentage of profits will be distributed as a **dividend** to each shareholder.
- Most businesses are likely to retain some profit in the business as a safeguard against possible poor profits, or even losses, in future years.

ONLINE

PROGRESS CHECK 18: Visit www.brightredbooks.net/N5BusMgmt and test your knowledge of trading and profit and loss accounts.

ONLINE TEST

How well have you learned this topic? Take the 'Trading and profit and loss account' test at www.brightredbooks.net/N5BusMgmt

HOW TO AVOID MAKING A LOSS

If a business is making a loss – which means that its costs are greater than its turnover (sales) – it can be the result of several factors. Businesses must use their **Trading and Profit and Loss Account** to help them make decisions about how to improve the future profitability of the business. The table outlines some of the reasons why a business makes a loss and the action that can be taken to address these.

Reason for loss	Action to be taken
Selling price of stock is too low	Increase selling price, but don't make it too high or the business will lose customers and sales will, therefore, fall.
Purchase price of stock is too high	Look for a cheaper supplier, but do not sacrifice on quality, or the business will lose customers and sales will, therefore, fall.
Too much stock left over at the end of the year	The business should undertake market research to ensure that they are purchasing stock that is popular with their customers.
Expenses are too high	Find ways to control expenses – for example, encourage employees to limit phone calls and use email instead, switch off lights or heaters when they are not required and find more cost-effective ways to promote and advertise products.

 **ACTIVITY: PREPARE AND INTERPRET A TRADING AND PROFIT AND LOSS ACCOUNT**

Prepare three Trading and Profit and Loss Accounts for three different sole traders. You can complete these manually (on paper and using a calculator) or you can use a spreadsheet to complete each activity.

Tracey Turner

From the information listed below, draw up the Trading and Profit and Loss Account for Tracey Turner for the year ended 31 December 200X.

	£
Sales	1700
Purchases	820
Opening stock	25
Closing stock	60
Insurance	25
Wages	32
Electricity	24

R Burton

From the information listed below, draw up the Trading and Profit and Loss Account for R Burton for the year ended 31 December 200X.

	£
Sales	17033
Purchases	9101
Opening stock	3521
Closing stock	3171
Insurance	130
Wages	200
General expenses	34
Telephone	146
Advertising	180

E Taylor

From the information listed below, draw up the Trading and Profit and Loss Account for E Taylor for the year ended 31 December 200X.

	£
Sales	50000
Opening stock	4000
Closing stock	5000
Purchases	22500
Wages	2000
Advertising	6000
Heat and light	1050
General expenses	2100

Examine the trading profit and loss accounts that you have just prepared for Tracey Turner, R Burton and E Taylor. Suggest two strategies that all of these businesses could use to improve their net profit.

 ## THINGS TO DO AND THINK ABOUT

Businesses produce a Trading and Profit and Loss Account at the end of their financial year. Think about stakeholders who might be interested in a Trading and Profit and Loss Account and why they would be interested in this financial information.

MANAGEMENT OF MARKETING AND OPERATIONS

CUSTOMERS

WHAT IS A MARKET?

A **market** is a place where **buyers** and **sellers** come together. A market does not have to be a physical place – for example, a lot of buying and selling now takes place on the internet.

 **ACTIVITY**

The table below consists of two columns. Column A identifies a **specific market**. In column B, you should give an example of a **seller** who operates within this market. The first two have been completed for you.

Column A	Column B
Name of market	**Example of seller within this market**
The clothing market	River Island and New Look
The housing market	Wimpey Homes
The food market	
The holiday market	
The car market	
The newspaper market	
The fast food market	
The computer market	
The mobile phone market	
The public transport market	

When consumers buy products, they do so with the aim of maximising their satisfaction and enjoyment. Sellers aim to earn a profit when they sell their goods and services in the market place to these consumers.

WHAT IS MARKETING?

Marketing is more than just advertising or selling a product. Marketing is about ensuring that the business meets the demands, needs and wants of customers in a market. This is how businesses survive and grow, and is known as the **marketing concept**.

This means that businesses need to find out what consumers want, and make a product that they will like and buy.

marketing

↓

Identify customer wants

↓

Anticipate customer requirements

↓

Attempt to satisfy these requirements

THE ROLE AND IMPORTANCE OF MARKETING

The purpose of marketing is to:

- help to raise awareness of products and services on offer
- help to raise the organisation's profile and image in the market
- encourage customers to purchase products
- target new customers
- retain existing customers
- help the business to identify changes and tastes in the market
- increase profits
- increase market share.

 **ONLINE**

TASK 33: Visit www.brightredbooks.net/N5BusMgmt and work out what message each organisation is trying to convey to its customers.

MARKET SEGMENTATION

Market segmentation involves splitting consumers into different groups and then marketing a product/service directly to those groups.

Consumers can be grouped in many ways such as:

1	Social class	2	Age
3	Family lifestyle	4	Occupation
5	Income	6	Gender
7	Geographical location	8	Religion

Market segmentation can be useful to an organisation because:

- the organisation can develop products that meet the needs of specific consumers
- appropriate prices can be set, which specific consumers can afford to pay but still allow the organisation to earn a profit
- appropriate promotions and advertising can be developed to target specific consumers
- it will ensure that products and services are sold in the appropriate location/places for the targeted consumers.

TARGET MARKETING

Differentiated marketing

This involves targeting **each market segment** with a product or service specifically designed to match the needs of those consumers within the segment. Many car manufacturers do exactly this by providing different cars for different consumers – for example, the Ford Focus is aimed at consumers with young children, whereas the Mazda MX5 is aimed at single people or couples with no children.

Undifferentiated or mass marketing

This involves selling products or services to the whole market. It is used as a strategy where the organisation assumes that consumers' needs are similar if not identical. Manufacturers of TV sets usually target the whole market.

ONLINE

TASK 34: Visit www. brightredbooks.net/ N5BusMgmt and complete the logo task.

ONLINE

TASK 35: Visit www. brightredbooks.net/ N5BusMgmt and complete the market segmentation task.

ONLINE

TASK 36: Visit www. brightredbooks.net/ N5BusMgmt and identify products or services that are mass marketed.

CASE STUDY

Turn to p91 and read case study 10, on DoggyChocs, then answer the questions.

ONLINE TEST

How well have you learned this topic? Try the 'Role of marketing' test at www.brightredbooks.net/ N5BusMgmt

THINGS TO DO AND THINK ABOUT

Here are two activities to test your knowledge of market segmentation and marketing.

Below is a list of well-known products. Which market segment are these products targeting? Record your answers in the table below.

Product/service	Which market segment are these products targeting?
Kellogg's CocoPops	
The Scotsman newspaper	
Mercedes cars	
Robinson's Fruit Shoot	
Remington hair straighteners	
Ralph Lauren aftershave	
Bupa residential nursing care	

In addition to using logos, some companies also use straplines or slogans. These are memorable phrases that communicate a product's appeal.

To the right is a list of well-known straplines. In the space provided write the name of the organisation **or** product that is being referred to.

No	Strapline/slogan	Organisation/product
1	'Just do it'	
2	'Because I'm worth it'	
3	'Every little helps'	
4	'It's not just food, it's ____ food'	
5	'The ultimate driving machine'	

MARKET RESEARCH 1

WHAT IS MARKET RESEARCH?

Market research involves the constant gathering, recording and analysing of data about an organisation's product/services and its target market. If a business doesn't meet the demands, needs and wants of its customers, it will probably fail.

Market research can help a business answer the following questions:

- How large is the market?
- How fast is the market growing?
- Are there any existing competitors and what share of the market do they hold?
- What makes consumers buy certain products?
- What prices are consumers prepared to pay for certain products?
- Are there any gaps in the market for the introduction of new products?

METHODS OF MARKET RESEARCH

There are two basic types of market research – **desk research** and **field research**

Desk research

Desk research involves looking at information that has already been gathered and analysed, for example from websites, newspapers, trade magazines and books.

Here, researchers use secondary information in the form of published sources – for example, the internet; government department reports; market research reports published by companies such as Keynote; competitors' websites; voters' roles and trade magazines.

This information has been gathered for one purpose and is then used for another.

contd

Field research

Here, researchers go out 'into the field' to obtain first-hand, primary information for the organisation to use.

This way of gathering new, up-to-date information can be very time-consuming and expensive to carry out.

ADVANTAGES OF DESK RESEARCH

- The information is usually easy to obtain because someone or some organisation has already undertaken the research.

- Because the research has already been undertaken, it is much cheaper than undertaking field research and so the organisation could save a lot of money.

- The organisation can react to market changes really quickly because the information is readily available.

DISADVANTAGES OF DESK RESEARCH

- The information is not as reliable as information obtained from field research due to the fact that the information was probably collected for another purpose, or for use by another organisation

- The information could be out of date if it was collected some time ago, and so it might not be relevant to today's market.

- If the information is inaccurate or biased, then it could lead to wrong decisions being made.

 ONLINE

TASK 37: Visit www. brightredbooks.net/ N5BusMgmt and complete the table.

ONLINE TEST

How well have you learned this topic? Take the 'Market research' test at www.brightredbooks.net/ N5BusMgmt

 ## THINGS TO DO AND THINK ABOUT

Visit one of the following websites:

Just-auto (www.just-auto.com)
Just-drinks (www.just-drinks.com)
Just-food (www.just-food.com)
Just-style (fashion) (www.just-style.com)

All four pull together news and market research in their particular sector. The market research comes from a wide range of suppliers and can be purchased online. The news is free and RSS (Really Simple Syndication) feeds of the news headlines are available.

MARKET RESEARCH 2

DIFFERENT METHODS OF FIELD RESEARCH

There are nine main methods of field research. We'll have a look at what each method involves, along with its advantages and disadvantages.

Personal interview

This is a face-to-face interview held in the street or in the customer's home.

Advantages:
- It allows two-way communication.
- The researcher can encourage the respondent to answer.
- Mistakes and misunderstandings can be dealt with.

Disadvantages:
- It takes a lot of time and can be expensive.
- Home interviews tend to be unpopular with consumers.

Telephone survey

This involves a market researcher telephoning people at home and asking them questions.

Advantages:
- It's relatively inexpensive.
- The response is immediate.
- A large number of people can be surveyed very quickly.

Disadvantages:
- Many people don't like strangers phoning them up and asking questions.
- Some people refuse to talk and just hang up.

Postal survey

This involves a market researcher sending a questionnaire out through the post.

Advantages:
- It's inexpensive, as it doesn't require a trained interviewer.

Disadvantages:
- Questions must be simple and easy to answer.
- The response rate is very low, as people tend to bin them as 'junk mail'.
- Free gifts have to be offered as an incentive to encourage people to complete them.

Electronic/online survey

As more and more homes have internet access, more businesses are using ICT and the internet to reach their customers and carry out market research. Electronic/online surveys involve creating and then sending a questionnaire via email to consumers.

Advantages:
- It's inexpensive.
- It can have a quick and healthy response rate.

Disadvantages:
- The responses might be too brief for them to be meaningful.
- There is little control over **who** answers some of the questionnaires, and so some returns are useless.

Focus group

This involves specially selected groups of people and is led by an experienced chairperson who puts forward points to encourage discussion.

Advantages:
- This provides an opportunity to collect qualitative information in the form of opinions, feelings and attitudes.

Disadvantages:
- Qualitative information can be very difficult to analyse.

Hall test

This is where a product is given to customers to try and their feedback is obtained.

Advantages:
- Customers actually try the product and so can give good feedback.
- It's fairly inexpensive to carry out.

Disadvantages:
- Customers might feel obliged to give positive feedback because they've had a free product.
- It can be difficult to analyse qualitative information.

contd

Observation

This involves watching something and recording what happens – it could be that the observer has to count how many times something happens. For example, a restaurant owner might want to observe diners' responses to a new and improved menu.

Advantages:
- The people being observed are probably oblivious to this fact and will therefore respond in a natural way.
- Quantitative information is gathered. This is easier to analyse than qualitative information.

Disadvantages:
- The observer can't ask those being observed to explain why they did or did not do something.

Sampling*

It's impossible to survey everybody, so you have to select a sample. This can be done randomly.

Advantages:
- It is relatively quick to carry out.
- It is relatively inexpensive.

Disadvantages:
- The sample chosen might not be representative of everyone, so it could be inaccurate.

*Sampling can be done **randomly** using people from the electoral role. Alternatively, **quota sampling** can be used, where the interviewer only selects people who meet certain criteria such as age or gender.

Electronic Point of Sale (EPOS)

This method is used by retailers when a loyalty card is swiped through their electronic tills. They gather information about customers' shopping habits in this way. Tesco use a club card system to find out what their customers want and to try to gain their loyalty.

Advantages:
- It can give accurate consumer profiles.
- It allows retailers to offer promotions tailored to consumers' needs.

Disadvantages:
- It can be very expensive to set up.
- It is time-consuming to set up.

ONLINE

TASK 38 and 39: Visit www.brightredbooks.net/N5BusMgmt and undertake the market research tasks.

ONLINE

PROGRESS CHECK 19: Visit www.brightredbooks.net/N5BusMgmt and test your knowledge of market research.

ONLINE TEST

How well have you learned this topic? Take the 'Market research' test at www.brightredbooks.net/N5BusMgmt

ADVANTAGES OF FIELD RESEARCH

- Information can be gathered for a specific purpose – e.g., a survey to find out about consumers' shopping habits.
- Information is relevant – it can be linked directly to a product or particular services or shops.
- Research can focus on what a business specifically wants to find out.
- Interviewers can explain questions to those being surveyed.
- Information gathered is up to date.

DISADVANTAGES OF FIELD RESEARCH

- It can be very costly to set up.
- It can take a great deal of time and expense to train interviewers.
- A wide audience must be surveyed if the findings are to be realistic.
- Information needs to be analysed and interpreted after it has been collected.
- There is no guarantee that the views of those sampled reflect those of the whole country.
- The way questions are worded or asked can influence people's responses.

THINGS TO DO AND THINK ABOUT

Explain the meaning of the following words/terms:

Word	Definition/meaning
Field research	
Qualitative information	
Quantitative information	
Primary information	
Secondary information	

THE MARKETING MIX 1

OVERVIEW

Marketing involves identifying consumer needs and wants and attempting to satisfy them. For any product to be marketed successfully, the business must decide on the correct marketing mix – sometimes referred to as the **four Ps**:

- Product
- Price
- Place
- Promotion

Product	The product/service that the customer purchases. The product includes the packaging, image, guarantee and the after-sales service – for example, carrying out repairs.
Price	The actual amount set by the seller, and paid by the customer to the seller.
Place	Where the customer purchases the product/service.
Promotion	The way in which a customer is made aware of a product/service and is persuaded to buy it. Promotion includes advertising and sales promotion.

We'll now look at each of these factors in turn.

DON'T FORGET

Getting product, price, place and promotion right is the key to marketing success!

PRODUCT

A product is a good or service that is sold to consumers. Consumers buy a product because it meets a need and/or satisfies a want. If a product is to be successful, it must meet the needs and/or wants of the consumer.

A product is said to have three elements.

Augmented product
These are the additional extras which add to the value of the product in the eyes of the consumer – for example, extended warranties, free road tax and insurance and after-sales service.

Actual product
This is the tangible or physical product and includes the colour, style and quality. For example, a car is the actual product you purchase and drive.

Core product
What the product actually does: its main function, and so, what makes it useful for the consumer. For example, a car is useful to the consumer because it's a convenient method of transport.

3 elements of a product

PRODUCT MIX

A firm's product mix is the range of products that it produces. For example, Baxters Food Group has a product mix which includes jams, sauces and soups.

By identifying the stage in the **product life cycle** of each of their products, a business can plan when to introduce new products as old products go into decline.

Most businesses will have a range of products to spread the risk of one product failing. If a firm only produced one product and it failed, the whole business could fail. In addition, a wide range of products can:

- meet the needs of different market segments
- increase profits
- increase the status and reputation of the firm.

EXTENSION

The sections on augmented products, product mix and product orientation are all extension knowledge which will be useful if you go on to study for Higher Business Management.

PRODUCT ORIENTATION

Firms with a product-orientated (or asset-led) approach to marketing and selling try to sell whatever they can make without trying to find out if it's what the consumers want. They simply look at the assets and strengths of their business to determine what products they should make and sell. Apple is a good example of a business that has had great success in a long line of product-led launches. Apple has focused on the product rather than the wants of the customer!

ONLINE

TASK 40: Visit www.brightredbooks.net/N5BusMgmt and do the product mix task.

MARKET ORIENTATION

An organisation with a market-orientated approach (or a market-led organisation) thinks that its most important asset is its customers. The firm believes that, as long as it is able to identify potential customers, find out what they want, and then produce that for them, it will remain successful.

BRANDING

A **brand** is a name, symbol, design (or a combination of all these) that the producer uses to make the product instantly recognisable.

A brand can relate to a specific product – for example, Irn Bru. It can also refer to the whole company – for example, Heinz.

Once a brand has been established, the business has to work hard to maintain its high public profile.

Some brands are so powerful that they are generally used to describe a product. For example, most consumers simply refer to correction fluid as Tipp-Ex, vacuum cleaners as Hoovers and sticky tape as Sellotape. There are many varieties of these products on the market, but market leaders have been so successful at branding, that these products are simply known by the brand name.

THE ADVANTAGES OF SUCCESSFUL BRANDING

There are a number of advantages to establishing a successful brand:

- A business can save money on marketing once the product becomes a household name.
- Higher prices can be charged when consumers become loyal to the brand.
- It is easier to launch new products or new versions of products with the same brand name.

However, some brands – especially clothing and expensive accessories – are relatively easy to copy, so fake versions can appear on the market. This can be expensive for a business to fight against!

On the other hand, a poor brand can affect the whole range of products produced by the same manufacturer.

A well-known brand might be seen as a guarantee of high quality. Some brands are easily recognisable and there can be an element of 'snob value' in a consumer using them.

 THINGS TO DO AND THINK ABOUT

Using the table below, list some well-known branded products which you (and perhaps other consumers) consider to be high quality and show expensive taste. An example has been completed for you.

1	Vans (shoes)	2	
3		4	
5		6	
7		8	

Some loyal consumers are likely to be less sensitive to price increases as they refuse to buy rival products even if they are significantly cheaper.

 ONLINE TEST

How well have you learned this topic? Take the 'Product' test at www.brightredbooks.net/N5BusMgmt

THE MARKETING MIX 2

PRODUCT LIFE CYCLE

The product life cycle shows the different stages that a new product passes through during its life, and the sales that can be expected at each of these stages. There are generally four stages in any product life cycle:

Introduction

Growth

Maturity

Decline

DON'T FORGET

The four stages of the product life cycle are introduction, growth, maturity and decline.

DON'T FORGET

A business has to invest time and money to ensure that consumers become aware of a new product.

DON'T FORGET

As consumers' knowledge of the product grows, so do sales.

DON'T FORGET

As the market becomes saturated with the product, competition becomes fierce and prices fall.

DON'T FORGET

Consumer tastes change, sales fall, prices become low and the product is withdrawn.

Product Life Cycle Diagram
All products have a life span – just like us

Introduction	Growth	Maturity	Decline
Sales are low. Profits will be negative.	Sales increase rapidly. Profits will reach their highest point at the end of this stage.	Sales reach their highest point. Profits will begin to fall as competition increases.	Sales are falling. Profits continue to fall and may become negative.

Sales

Time

Introduction

The product is first launched on the market. Costs of advertising and promoting the product will probably be high at this stage because the business has to invest time and money ensuring that the consumer becomes aware of the new product. If the product is unique, there will be few competitors and usually the product will command a high price.

Growth

Sales are increasing steadily as consumers' knowledge of the product grows. A few competitors might launch their own versions of the product. These competitors could pose a threat to the business.

Maturity

The product becomes commonplace in the market and growth of sales start to slow down as competition from other firms increases. As the market becomes saturated, competition becomes fierce and prices tumble. One example of this would be DVD players – there are so many versions of these on the market now that the price has fallen dramatically.

Decline

Consumer tastes change, technology develops and new, more advanced products are launched. Consumers are no longer impressed by the product, and they stop buying it. Sales fall, prices become very low and eventually the product is withdrawn from the market because it is no longer profitable. Examples of this include videos/video recorders and typewriters.

The length of the product life cycle depends on the product. Car models have a life cycle of approximately five years, clothes fashions often have a life cycle of a few months and CD singles tend to have a life cycle of a few weeks.

Some products, such as Mars Bars, Persil washing powder, Heinz Baked Beans and Coca Cola, appear never to have reached the decline stage.

This is because they have:

- used successful extension strategies
- employed constant brand promotion
- developed a strong brand loyalty from their customers
- no close rivals
- established high status and a good reputation in the market.

NEW PRODUCT DEVELOPMENT

The Marketing Department will always be looking for a 'gap' in the market to launch a new product. Before a new product can be launched the Marketing Department will:

- undertake market research to identify a list of new potential products

- consider if it has enough finance and resources to develop a new product

- develop a prototype of what the new product might look like

- test the product with potential customers and if feedback is positive, promote and advertise the product prior to its launch.

 THINGS TO DO AND THINK ABOUT

Here is an activity to test your knowledge of the product life cycle:

Activity

Using the graph paper provided, draw a diagram showing the product life cycle. Remember to label all the parts of your diagram correctly.

The product life cycle

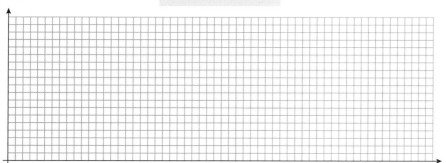

THE MARKETING MIX 3

PRICE

The price of a product or service must be set at a level that consumers are willing to pay, meet all the costs of the business and also enable the business to make a profit.

All businesses need to remember that price affects sales. Lowering the price might increase consumer demands but if the price is set too low, consumers could think it is a lower quality product.

It is also important to look at the prices that competitors are charging, particularly in more competitive markets. Most businesses set their prices to be in line with, or slightly lower than, competitors in an attempt to attract them to their product instead. Both Asda and Tesco manufacture their own brands of baked beans. There is no difference in price for these products.

Overall, the price a business charges for a product should be based on what the consumer is prepared to pay for it. Other factors that will be taken into account when setting price are:

- the aims of the business. For example, is the aim to maximise profits? If so, price is likely to be high

- prices charged by competitors

- the position of the product in its life cycle – at the decline stage, price is usually lower

- the time of year – is the product seasonal? For example, strawberries are usually much cheaper in the summer

- the place where the product is sold. For example, businesses often lower prices if consumers buy on the internet

- the market segment the product is aimed at. For example, some cars are designed, manufactured and marketed at lower income consumers.

PRICING STRATEGIES

Penetration pricing is used when a business wants to enter a market where there are lots of competitors selling similar products. The firm will set its price very low (below the price of competitors) when it enters the market. Once the business and its product become popular with customers, it will then raise its prices.

Destroyer pricing is used to eliminate the competition. Prices are lowered to such a degree that some competitors cannot compete and are forced to leave the market. Once out of the market, the dominant firm raises price again.

contd

In the case of **promotional pricing**, prices are reduced for a short period of time to shift goods off the shelves that may not be selling as fast as the business would like.

Premium pricing is when high prices for a product are set and kept high to create a high class image. The product is being marketed to consumers with a high income and an 'eye for quality'.

Competitive pricing is a strategy that encourages businesses in the same market to charge the same or similar prices – this prevents a price war. The firms deliberately agree not to compete on price. Instead, they compete through advertising and offering free gifts, for example. Supermarkets and petrol stations sometimes use this strategy.

Price discrimination is when a business charges different prices for the same product or service at different times of the year or day. For example, Thomas Cook increase the cost of holidays during June to August and then lower them around October time. BT charge higher prices for phone calls during the day than they charge for phone calls made in the evening.

Sometimes a business will sell some of its products at a loss. This is known as **loss leaders**. The aim is to attract customers into the store. It is hoped that customers will then spend money buying other products and so the business will still make an overall profit.

Market skimming is when a business puts a new product on the market at a high price. The business aims to make a really high profit to cover the cost of researching and designing the product. However, once competition enters the market, prices will then be forced back down. This tends to be used with electronic products such as iPads.

EXTENSION

This section on pricing strategies is extension knowledge which will be useful if you go on to study for Higher Business Management.

THINGS TO DO AND THINK ABOUT

In this activity you have to compare the prices of everyday household groceries sold by three well-known supermarkets.

- Use the internet to find the price that each supermarket sells the product at.
- Record your answers on the table.
- In the last column, calculate the difference between the highest and lowest price offered.

ONLINE

PROGRESS CHECK 21: Visit www.brightredbooks.net/N5BusMgmt and test your knowledge of pricing strategies.

ONLINE TEST

How well have you learned this topic? Take the 'Price' test at www.brightredbooks.net/N5BusMgmt

Product	Asda price	Tesco price	Morrisons price	Price difference
Fairy Liquid				
Kellogg's Cornflakes				
Innocent Orange Juice				
Nescafe Coffee				

THE MARKETING MIX 4

PLACE

ONLINE

TASK 41: Visit www.
brightredbooks.net/
N5BusMgmt and take part in
a discussion.

This is the process by which the product reaches the market and, ultimately, the consumer. A business has to decide on the most cost-effective way to make its products easily available to consumers. This is sometimes referred to as the channel of distribution.

A product can reach the consumer by following three main routes:

1 Manufacturer ——————→ Customer

2 Manufacturer ——————→ Retailer ——————→ Customer

3 Manufacturer ——————→ Wholesaler ——————→ Retailer ——————→ Customer

WHAT CHANNEL OF DISTRIBUTION SHOULD A BUSINESS USE?

This depends on a number of factors:

The Product
Where a product is designed and made to meet a customer's special requirements, it will normally be sold directly from the manufacturer to the customer. Where products are mass produced, like food products, they will normally reach the customer after passing through a wholesaler and retailer.

Reliability
When a wholesaler or retailer proves to be unreliable, the manufacturer might decide to sell directly to the customer and cut out the 'middle-men'.

Distribution capability
If the manufacturer does not possess a strong and well-trained sales team and suitable delivery vans, then they might have to distribute their products through a wholesaler or retailer.

Finance
The preferred option is when manufacturers have sufficient money to develop their own channel of distribution. However, when money is limited, they are more likely to distribute their goods and services to consumers through a wholesaler or retailer.

EXTENSION

This section on channels of
distribution, and the section
on retailing (page 69) are
both extension knowledge
which will be useful if you
go on to study for Higher
Business Management.

OTHER CHANNELS OF DISTRIBUTION

Internet (e-commerce)
Many business organisations sell their goods and services using the internet. Customers make payments using their debit or credit card. This allows businesses to reach customers all over the world. Businesses devote a lot of time and money designing attractive websites.

Telesales
There has been a rapid growth in the use of call centres by many businesses. Cold calling is a method of direct communication that allows a business to reach customers and market their products without using a high street retailer.

Mail order
Many businesses also use mail order. They invest money in glossy catalogues and consumers can then place orders directly with the business. This often reduces the cost of distribution as fewer shops and staff are required.

contd

Newspaper and magazine selling

Some businesses advertise their products in newspapers and magazines and give consumers the opportunity to complete coupons, which they can send to the company to order goods and services.

Delivery methods

A business must also consider the best method of physically transporting finished products from the business to the customer. For example, should they use road rail, air or sea etc.? Choosing the most efficient method of transport should ensure a business's output reaches the market place (customer) on time and at the most appropriate cost to the business.

INFLUENCES ON LOCATION

When choosing a location for a business, there are certain points to consider which can affect its success or failure. These include:

- availability of labour
- availability of capital
- infrastructure – that is, rail and road links
- government loans and grants
- European Union grants
- distance to market

- source of raw materials
- health and safety
- rival businesses
- telecommunications – for example, fibre optic and broadband
- transport costs
- information costs.

DON'T FORGET

A business which locates successfully can achieve higher sales, lower costs and high profits.

RETAILING TRENDS

There has been a big increase recently in out-of-town shopping with the development of huge retail parks. This provides convenience for both consumers and sellers – it is good to have all the shops you might need under the one roof.

Many retail parks now have extended opening hours, late into the evening and indeed many supermarkets are open 24/7.

Supermarkets are now extending their product mix to include petrol, pharmacy, photography, and opticians.

Most retailers now use the internet to encourage online shopping.

ONLINE

TASK 42: Visit www.brightredbooks.net/N5BusMgmt and take part in the discussion about location.

ONLINE TEST

How well have you learned this topic? Take the 'Place' test at www.brightredbooks.net/N5BusMgmt

 THINGS TO DO AND THINK ABOUT

Discuss the following questions with a friend.

1 Why do you think nuclear power stations have to consider where they locate?

2 Why is it important to consider availability of labour before deciding on location?

3 What factors should a coffee shop consider before choosing a location?

4 What telecommunications factors should a business consider before moving to a new location?

Take another look at the list under 'Influences on location'. Consider the points below and decide which factors they are describing or relate to.

1 This business requires a great deal of raw materials – for example, a steel works.

2 Does the local workforce have the correct skills required?

3 There is a gap in the market as no other firm supplies this product.

4 Is there good access to motorways, train lines and airports which will make it easier to transport goods?

5 Are there any government incentives in a particular area?

A nuclear power station

THE MARKETING MIX 5

PROMOTION

This is how the business informs the consumers about their products and how they persuade them to purchase the products.

PROMOTIONAL STRATEGIES

There are a number of promotional strategies that a business can use:

Advertising	Advertising is about letting people know that a product exists and trying to persuade them to buy it. It is used to inform people about the product, how much it costs and what it does. Without advertising, people wouldn't know that a product exists.
Special offers	Discounts provide customers with money off a product when they buy it. Special offers can include, for example, a 20 per cent discount, three items for the cost of two or buy-one-get-one-free (BOGOF).
Free samples	Some businesses give out free samples or tasters of products to see if people like them. If they do like them, they might decide to buy the products. For example, some perfume shops give out free samples of perfumes for people to try. Without the free samples, customers might never know if they liked them!
Celebrity endorsement	A celebrity is used to promote a business and its products. For example, Jamie Oliver has been used to promote Sainsbury's.

TYPES OF ADVERTISING

Advertising is just one of the ways that a business can create publicity around their products/services. There are four main types of advertising:

Informative adverts	These are used to inform the consumer about the good or service being sold.
Persuasive adverts	These are used to persuade customers to buy the good or service by giving the impression that it is desirable to own these products or use these services.
Product endorsement	This is where celebrities or sports professionals are paid to wear and use products. For example, Adidas pay David Beckham to wear their products.
Product placement	This is when a business pays for its product to appear in a movie or TV programme – for example, James Bond drives a BMW Z8 in the film *The World is Not Enough*.

METHODS OF ADVERTISING

The following table shows the advantages and disadvantages of the main methods of advertising.

Media	Advantages	Disadvantages
TV	You can reach many consumers. You can demonstrate the product. Regular adverts will increase the profile of the product.	Very expensive. Many viewers 'channel hop' during the adverts. The advert might not have to be seen by all consumers (market segments).
Newspapers	You can reach many consumers. Products can be aimed at certain consumers (market segments) by choosing the correct paper. Readers can cut out and complete coupons.	Adverts are often in black and white. Can be expensive if placed in newspapers with a large circulation.

contd

Magazines	Often in colour and have a better impact. Can target certain consumers (market segments) by advertising in certain magazines. Magazines are usually kept for future reference.	Can be expensive to advertise in magazines. Competitors will usually also be advertising in these magazines.
Radio	Much cheaper than TV. Captive audience as listeners tend not to 'channel hop' during adverts.	Listeners often do not pay attention during the adverts. Sound only, listeners cannot see the product and have to use their imagination.
Cinema	Captive audience, can't 'channel hop' or avoid the advert.	Limited audience. Consumers tend to remember the film rather than the advert.
Direct mail	Relatively cheap. Can target particular consumers (market segments).	Many consumers tend to dislike 'junk mail' and destroy without reading.
Bill boards	Usually in busy locations so large audience. Passers-by will frequently see the advert.	Deteriorate quickly due to the weather. Often suffer from vandalism.
Internet	Relatively cheap. Adverts can be changed and updated quickly. Adverts can target certain consumers (market segments).	Web surfers tend to ignore adverts.
Apps More organisations are now using Apps to advertise and promote products.	They can be downloaded onto a phone and consumers can use the app when they are on the move.	A smart phone is usually required. Staff require training on how to design an app that is consumer friendly.

The choice of advertising media depends on the:

- product to be advertised
- consumers (market segment) to be targeted
- type of coverage required – for example, is the product to be sold locally or nationally?
- finance available to the business for advertising
- method of advertising used by competitors
- legal restrictions – for example, tobacco products cannot be advertised on TV.

CASE STUDY

Turn to p91, read case study 10 (Juicebox) and answer the questions.

ONLINE

TRIAL ASSESSMENT: put what you have learned about marketing to the test in this trial assessment.

ETHICAL MARKETING

Ethics are moral guidelines which encourage good behaviour. Behaving ethically is doing what is morally correct. An ethical decision is one that is both legal and meets the shared ethical standards of the community. It would not be ethical for a business to:

- deliberately market their products at vulnerable groups, for example, children or the elderly
- obtain research data illegally or without permission
- exclude potential customers from the market
- reach agreements with competitors to keep prices high, and so exploit customers to earn as much profit as possible.

There is now an expectation that all businesses will be socially responsible and support good causes.

ONLINE TEST

How well have you learned this topic? Take the 'Promotion' test at www.brightredbooks.net/N5BusMgmt

EXAMPLE

Green and Blacks, a UK based chocolate company, submitted its Maya Gold Chcolate line to the Fair Trade certification process for its partnership with the Toledo Cacao Growers Association of Belize.

THINGS TO DO AND THINK ABOUT

To be successful, a business must ensure that it has an effective marketing mix – product, price, place and promotion. You can work with a friend or on your own to complete this task.

1. You should prepare an eight-slide PowerPoint presentation which demonstrates your knowledge and understanding of the marketing mix.

2. You should present your presentation to the class.

3. Insert your name in the footer of your presentation (notes and handouts), print out a copy and store in your work folder.

SUPPLIERS

DECIDING ON A SUPPLIER

The factors that need to be considered when deciding on a supplier is known as the **purchasing mix**. The choice of which supplier to use will depend on a number of factors:

Raw materials

These are the 'ingredients' needed to make a product. For example, a business that manufactures chocolate bars would have to purchase the following raw materials from one or more suppliers:

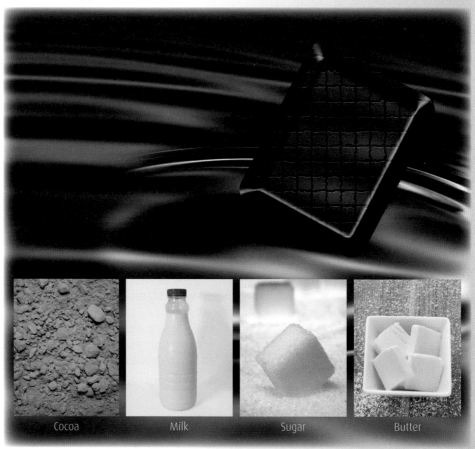

Cocoa | Milk | Sugar | Butter

Price

If a business aims to earn a profit, then the cost of purchasing stock needs to be kept to a minimum. The business should source a supplier that can offer a competitive price for supplies.

Quality

The business cannot sacrifice quality. If raw materials are not of a high quality, it is likely that the finished products produced by the business will also be of poor quality. In addition, there could be a lot of wastage as a result of using poor quality raw materials.

Suppliers should be able to guarantee the same high quality each time an order is placed, because the finished product needs to be of a consistent quality for customers.

contd

Quantity

When large amounts of stock are to be purchased, the business should seek suppliers who are able to offer trade discounts for bulk buying or for loyal custom.

Reliability

It could be very costly to the business if the supplier is not able to deliver on time. Production could stop and customers will be unhappy if products are not available or delivery dates are not met.

Delivery

Some raw materials are perishable and so will need to be ordered just prior to being used in production. The business doesn't want production to stop because the supplier cannot deliver on time.

Credit

Suppliers who can offer credit facilities for purchasing raw materials can be an attractive option. Buying on credit allows the business to purchase the raw materials, manufacture and sell their products and then make payment to the supplier. This can help the business's cash flow situation.

Location

Suppliers who are local (for example, in the same town) might be able to deliver much more quickly and at shorter notice. Transportation costs (delivery charges) are also likely to be much lower.

DON'T FORGET

It is essential that the correct suppliers are selected so that the organisation can produce quality products at the right price in the right place at the right time.

ONLINE

TASK 43: Head to www. brightredbooks.net/ N5BusMgmt and follow the 'Choosing and managing suppliers' link for a Business Scotland guide. It's an excellent resource - take time to read through it!

ONLINE TEST

How well have you learned this topic? Take the 'suppliers' test at www.brightredbooks.net/ N5BusMgmt

THINGS TO DO AND THINK ABOUT

1   Large organisations like McDonald's and Subway do not have contracts with any of their major suppliers. This allows them to change supplier at very short notice. What advantages does this arrangement offer these organisations?

2   Explain why it is important that a business purchases from a supplier who can offer competitive prices.

3   Outline the consequences for a business who sacrifices quality for low prices when selecting a supplier.

4   Explain why it is important that a business secures a supplier who can deliver on time.

5   State what is meant by the following terms:

   • bulk buying

   • trade discount.

6   What are the advantages of choosing a supplier who offers the opportunity to purchase on credit?

7   State what is meant by the term purchasing mix.

STOCK MANAGEMENT 1

WHAT IS 'OPERATIONS'?

Organisations use resources to make products. '**Operations**' is the name given to the process of turning raw materials into finished articles – products ready to be sold.

Today, most goods are produced using the production line method – labour and machinery are used to complete different stages of a product.

Depending on the type of product, there will be a mix of labour and machinery used to produce it. There are three main stages in the system of operations:

Input (Stage 1)		Process (Stage 2)		Output (Stage 3)
Raw materials are purchased and labour is employed	→	The production process commences	→	The finished product – ready for consumers to purchase

EXAMPLE:

Here's an example of the production process for car manufacturing.

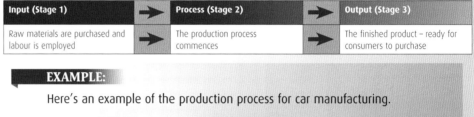

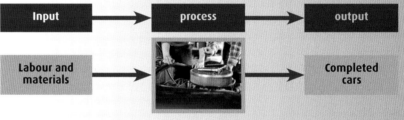

WHAT DOES THE OPERATIONS DEPARTMENT DO?

The role of the operations department involves:

STOCK MANAGEMENT

The operations department must control and manage stock levels to ensure that the correct quantity is available at all times to keep production going.

Careful decisions have to be taken about the quantity of raw materials or components to be bought, and which suppliers to use.

STOCK CONTROL

Stock levels should be recorded on **stock record cards** or held on a computer spreadsheet. These record stock used or issued to departments and received from suppliers. The balance on the stock record card should match the actual stock levels on the shelves.

contd

The operations department also has to consider four important factors relating to stock control:

- What is the **maximum stock** they should hold?
- What is the **minimum stock** they should hold?
- At what **level** should they **re-order** stock?
- What should the **re-order quantity** be?

Maximum stock

This is the level of stock that should be held for the organisation to minimise the costs of storing stock. When setting this level, the business should take into account the storage space available, security measures in place, cost of storage facilities – for example, employing warehouse staff – and the amount of finance (money) that will be tied up in stock. Money tied up in stock cannot be used for other things!

Minimum stock

A minimum stock level is the level that stock must not fall below as shortages in raw materials could result in reduced output and customers' orders not being met. When setting minimum stock levels, a business should take into account delivery times of their suppliers – for example, can they deliver next day?

Re-order level

This is the point at which new stock should be ordered. As items are taken from stock, the amount left for use reduces and, at some point, new stock has to be ordered. This is calculated by considering average daily usage and the time taken to receive new supplies (known as lead time).

Re-order quantity

Once the re-order level is reached, a standard quantity is automatically requested. When this new stock is received, the maximum stock level should be restored.

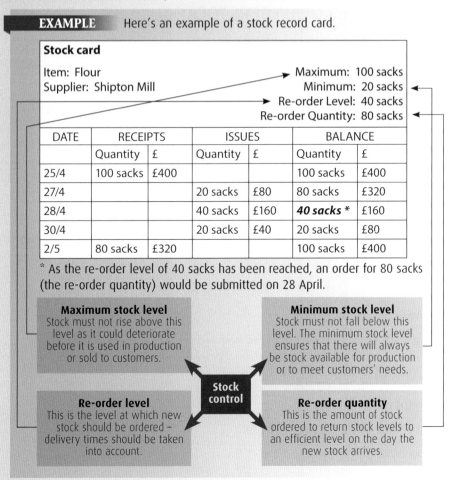

EXAMPLE   Here's an example of a stock record card.

Stock card

Item: Flour
Supplier: Shipton Mill

Maximum: 100 sacks
Minimum: 20 sacks
Re-order Level: 40 sacks
Re-order Quantity: 80 sacks

DATE	RECEIPTS		ISSUES		BALANCE	
	Quantity	£	Quantity	£	Quantity	£
25/4	100 sacks	£400			100 sacks	£400
27/4			20 sacks	£80	80 sacks	£320
28/4			40 sacks	£160	*40 sacks* *	£160
30/4			20 sacks	£40	20 sacks	£80
2/5	80 sacks	£320			100 sacks	£400

* As the re-order level of 40 sacks has been reached, an order for 80 sacks (the re-order quantity) would be submitted on 28 April.

Maximum stock level
Stock must not rise above this level as it could deteriorate before it is used in production or sold to customers.

Minimum stock level
Stock must not fall below this level. The minimum stock level ensures that there will always be stock available for production or to meet customers' needs.

Stock control

Re-order level
This is the level at which new stock should be ordered – delivery times should be taken into account.

Re-order quantity
This is the amount of stock ordered to return stock levels to an efficient level on the day the new stock arrives.

DON'T FORGET

It is important that a business has the right stock levels. If stock is too low, there is a danger that production could stop. Hold too much stock, and the business runs the risk of the stock going out of date.

VIDEO LINK

Check out the stock control video at www.brightredbooks.net/N5BusMgmt

ONLINE

TASK 44: Head to www.brightredbooks.net/N5BusMgmt and complete the stock card for Sand and Mortar, Building Merchants.

ONLINE

PROGRESS CHECK 22: Visit www.brightredbooks.net/N5BusMgmt and test your knowledge of stock management.

ONLINE TEST

How well have you learned this topic? Take the 'Stock management' test at www.brightredbooks.net/N5BusMgmt

THINGS TO DO AND THINK ABOUT

Technology plays an important part in stock control. Spreadsheet packages, such as Microsoft Excel, are used for recording stock movements. What are the advantages of using spreadsheets to record and update stock levels?

STOCK MANAGEMENT 2

DISADVANTAGES OF OVERSTOCKING

Overstocking has the following disadvantages:

- High storage costs – for example, warehouse staff might have to be employed.
- High security costs – for example, a security guard might have to be employed.
- High insurance costs, especially if stock has a high value.
- Large amounts of space would be required for storage.
- Money which could be used elsewhere in the business is tied up in stock.
- Stock could deteriorate, become obsolete or spoiled before it is used in production or sold to customers.
- There is also a danger of theft from employees.

DISADVANTAGES OF UNDERSTOCKING

Understocking also has its disadvantages:

- A business might not be able to cope with an unexpected order if stocks are low. This would upset customers who might take their business somewhere else.
- If the delivery of new stock is delayed, the business could run out of stock and production might have to stop. Customers could become dissatisfied.
- Holding low amounts of stock means firms have to place orders more often – this significantly increases administration costs. The firm might also lose out on discounts from bulk buying.
- A firm could gain a bad reputation if it can't satisfy customers' demands.

MANAGEMENT OF STOCK CONTROL

The three main ways of managing stock control are computerised stock control, intelligent stock control systems and **Just in Time production**.

Computerised stock control

Many organisations hold their stock details in a computer database or spreadsheet. This helps keep balances up to date after stock has been received and issued. Some are programmed to order more stock automatically as the re-order level is reached. Computerised stock control can be costly to set up and operate due to hardware, software and maintenance costs.

Computerised stock control – Argos

When you visit an Argos store you can check whether it has the item you want as the store has an up-to-the-minute computerised record of what it has in stock. Where stocks have fallen below a given level, an automatic re-order code is fed into Argos's distribution system so that it will be very unlikely to have items out of stock. This effective automated stock control system saves Argos millions of pounds simply by making sure the organisation never has too much or too few items in stock.

Another advantage of the system at Argos is that customers can actually check stock availability themselves!

contd

Intelligent stock control systems – supermarkets

Today, supermarkets such as Tesco and Asda use intelligent stock control systems to give them a competitive edge over their rivals. Supermarkets use **bar codes** to help with stock control. As each item is scanned at the checkout, it is taken from the recorded stock level. This allows the manager to check stock levels for each item of stock, total stock levels in the store, and the store's sales, easily at any time of the day. Best-selling items of stock and slow moving items can also be easily identified.

Supermarkets generally buy stocks on credit, perhaps paying for them a month or even longer after they have been delivered to their premises. By using automated stock control systems, they can get the stock on the shelves and into the customer's trolley almost immediately before they have even had to pay for them. The supermarket is never out of pocket.

Each item of stock will have its own unique bar code similar to the ones shown above.

As each product passes through the checkout, stock levels are automatically updated.

Just in Time production

Just in Time (JIT) production is a Japanese approach that keeps the stock levels (and therefore costs) to a minimum. Stock is ordered and arrives just in time to be used in production. Goods are **not** produced unless the firm has an order from a customer. To be successful, this system depends on:

- reliable suppliers
- good quality control.
- a team of committed and skilled workers

ONLINE TEST

How well have you learned this topic? Take the 'Stock management' test at www.brightredbooks.net/N5BusMgmt

THINGS TO DO AND THINK ABOUT

Sparky Electricians keep computerised records for all of their stock. Here is an extract from their stock records. Study this information and answer the questions below.

Explain what is meant by the following terms:

- Maximum stock level
- Minimum stock level.

Identify what items of stock listed above might have problems with current stock levels and state why?

Item	Max Stock Level	Min Stock Level	Stock in hand (Balance)
Welding Rods (50 pk)	150	50	30
Fuses (5 amp)	60	10	40
Fuses (3 amp)	80	15	70
Fuses (13 amp)	40	5	60
Ear plugs (pairs)	400	100	40
Safety Helmets	5	2	6
Safety goggles	20	4	2
Overalls (size 40)	4	2	1
Overalls (size 42)	4	2	3
Overalls (size 44)	4	2	3
Safety boots (size 8)	2	1	1
Safety boots (size 9)	2	1	2
Safety boots (size 10)	2	1	0

METHODS OF PRODUCTION

SYSTEM DESIGN: LAYOUT OF A FACTORY/PRODUCTION PROCESS

Operations managers have to decide on a layout of the factory/production process that will ensure the best and most efficient flow of work between different production areas. They also have to plan which staff are required and for what purpose, whether production will be labour intensive or capital intensive and what machinery and robots will be used.

Here is how a cake factory might be laid out to ensure a smooth production flow:

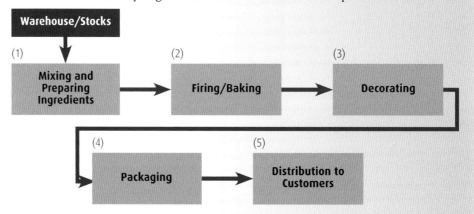

Warehouse/Stocks

(1) Mixing and Preparing Ingredients → (2) Firing/Baking → (3) Decorating

(4) Packaging → (5) Distribution to Customers

CAPITAL INTENSIVE PRODUCTION

Some companies like Coca-Cola employ very few people, but have high output levels because they are automated. This means that machines do the work instead of people. They use the latest computer-controlled equipment. These firms often produce items which are the same or very similar, and are known as capital intensive firms.

This method is used when:
- a standard product is being produced – like a two litre bottle of coca cola
- large scale production is required
- a high and consistent quality is required
- the product is more easily produced by machine rather than labour.

LABOUR INTENSIVE PRODUCTION

Other companies use humans rather than machinery to produce goods – particularly where a single product or a few of the same types of product are being produced – for example, designer dresses. This is known as the labour intensive system.

This method is used when:
- the product requires craftsmanship or special expertise
- standard, similar products are not being produced.

CAPITAL OR LABOUR INTENSIVE PRODUCTION?

The operations department has to decide on whether it wants to invest in machinery (**capital intensive production**) or humans (**labour intensive production**). It depends what is best for the business in the long run. Most manufacturing companies use a mixture of both.

Remember, employees who operate machines all day can find the work repetitive and boring and this leads to a lack of motivation.

Labour intensive	
Advantages	**Disadvantages**
Some manual labour is cheap to employ.	Skilled labour can be expensive to pay and train.
Some workers are highly skilled or offer expert craftsmanship.	Labour might only be suitable for small scale production. Labour on its own might not be able to mass produce.
Labour can be more suitable when the business cannot finance expensive machinery or equipment.	Staff absence could mean production stops and so orders might not be filled.

Capital intensive	
Advantages	**Disadvantages**
Machines are more efficient when a standard product is being produced.	Purchase, set-up costs and maintenance of machines can be very expensive.
Machines are more attractive when labour is scarce or expensive.	Lost production due to machine failures can be very costly to the business.
Machines are suitable for large scale production of identical items like Coca-Cola.	Individual customer specifications cannot be met as machines only produce standard products.

ONLINE

TASK 45: Visit www. brightredbooks.net/ N5BusMgmt and complete the table.

METHODS OF PRODUCTION

Production is the process in which raw materials, components and finished goods are converted into new goods or services. This can be done in different ways, depending on what is being produced.

Job production

Job production is where a single product is custom made to a customer's own specification. Kitchens, wedding cakes and wedding dresses are made using job production.

Advantages	Disadvantages
Firms can produce one-off orders to meet the customer's exact needs.	It's expensive to hire highly skilled staff.
High prices can usually be charged so high profits can be earned.	A wide variety of expensive tools, equipment and machines might be required.
Workers are more motivated as there is likely to be a variety of work and skills required.	One-off orders can take several months to complete, from the order being placed to delivery to the customer.

Batch production

Batch production is the production of groups of similar products. No item in a group goes on to the next stage until all are ready. For example, Heinz might produce a batch of soup, and all 20 000 cans of soup will be started in production, finished and distributed to customers at the same time.

Advantages	Disadvantages
All products in the batch are identical and so there should be no quality differences – all customers should receive exactly the same product.	Staff can be less motivated as they repeat the same task – batch after batch.
There is a reduced need for highly skilled and costly staff as work is broken down into simple stages and is fairly repetitive.	The business might have to purchase very expensive machinery, which can also be costly to maintain.
Machinery and robots can be used to complete a lot of the production, which can reduce costs in the long run.	Workers and machines might sit idle between batches of production if there is any fall in customer demand.

Flow Production

Flow production is a process in which the production of items moves continuously from one operation to the next. Each part of the process contributes to the eventual production of the final product. Usually, machinery or robots are employed to reduce labour costs. Products are produced to a standard specification. Examples would include the production of cars, soft drinks and TVs.

Advantages	Disadvantages
Huge quantities of goods can be produced.	Very expensive to purchase machinery and equipment.
Machinery can work 24/7.	Individual customer requirements cannot be met.
The process often makes use of machines and robots, which reduces labour costs and human mistakes.	Workers tend to find the jobs repetitive and so they become bored very quickly.
Because items are being produced in huge quantities, the costs can be spread over a great output which reduces the cost for the customer.	If machines break down or develop faults, production usually has to stop.

THINGS TO DO AND THINK ABOUT

Go to the following website: www.packagingnews.co.uk/tv/behind-scenes-at-tunnocks/ and read the article on Tunnock's packaging line. On a sheet of A4 paper, explain which part of their production process Tunnock's have decided to use machine-intensive production for, and why.

 ONLINE

TASK 46: Visit www. brightredbooks.net/ N5BusMgmt and provide the missing words.

QUALITY 1

OVERVIEW

What is a quality product? Most would agree that it has the following characteristics:

- uses high quality materials
- has a high standard of workmanship
- works well
- is reliable
- meets the specification stated on the packaging
- is environmentally friendly.

If a business develops and manufactures a quality product, it will probably find it easier to:

- satisfy customer demands
- meet safety standards and legal requirements
- ensure the product works properly or can be repaired easily
- charge a premium price
- achieve a high status and a good reputation in the market.

Business organisations in the UK use a variety of measures to ensure that their products/services meet a high level of quality. We'll look at these in more detail here.

QUALITY CONTROL PROCEDURES

A manufacturer passes a sample of raw materials and/or the final product through a quality control check. Any unacceptable products are then discarded as waste, or sent back for reworking.

Advantages:

- Substandard products are not sold to customers.
- The company is more likely to develop a good reputation if the quality of its products is consistently high.
- The company is, therefore, more likely to develop higher profits because it has more satisfied customers.

Disadvantages:

- More workers are needed to carry out quality control, and this costs time and money.

QUALITY ASSURANCE PROCEDURES

At certain points in the production process, products are checked to ensure that they meet agreed quality standards. All aspects of the production process are looked at to ensure errors do not occur. There is more emphasis on workers self-checking rather than checking by inspectors.

Advantages:

- Costs are reduced because there is less wastage, and there is no need to scrap completed poor-quality products – mistakes are spotted early on and dealt with!
- Staff motivation is improved because workers have more ownership and recognition of their work. Workers are encouraged to take pride in their own work.
- It can help break down 'us and them' barriers between workers and managers as it eliminates the feeling of workers being checked up on by managers.

BENCHMARKING

Identifying a benchmark – that is, identifying another organisation commonly regarded as the 'best' in the industry and copying their best techniques – is sometimes used as a method of improving the quality of production of a good or service.

Advantage:

- Setting a benchmark as a target can be very motivating for staff as it highlights the high standards to aim for.

Disadvantage:

- Companies must ensure that they continue to review their performance even after they have exceeded the benchmark.

QUALITY CIRCLES

These involve small groups of workers meeting at regular intervals to discuss where improvements can be made in the production process.

Advantage:

- Workers should become more motivated, more productive and more willing to introduce new production methods.

TOTAL QUALITY MANAGEMENT (TQM)

Total Quality Management is the most complete form of quality control. It tries to create a 'quality culture', encouraging everybody – from the Managing Director to the cleaners – to think about quality in everything they do. Every employee sets out to satisfy the customer. Customers are placed at the centre of the production process. Providing customers with the best quality product/service is the focus of every stage in the process, from the initial order to dispatch of the final good.

Advantages:

- Every worker is involved, so they feel responsible and can also be held accountable for their work.
- It establishes a 'quality culture', which ensures that quality is at the centre of everything the business does.

Disadvantages:

- It takes a lot of time to constantly check the standard of work at all stages of the production.
- All staff must be trained in TQM, which can be very costly for the business.

THINGS TO DO AND THINK ABOUT

1 Work with a friend to complete this activity.

2 Study the diagram to the right.

3 Discuss what you think is meant by each of the following terms:

- Quality control
- Methods of production
- Distribution of the final product
- Purchasing of raw materials.

| Purchasing of raw materials | Role of Operations | Quality control – ensuring final products are of a high standard |
| Managing the levels of stocks | Organising efficient methods of production | Storage and final distribution of the final product |

4 Once you have discussed each of the terms, complete the table below by writing a brief description of each term.

Term	Definition/meaning of term
Quality control	
Methods of production	
Distribution of the final product	
Purchasing of raw materials	

QUALITY 2

PURCHASING RAW MATERIALS

The first task for the operations department is to purchase the raw materials that the business requires to produce its product or service. The operations department must buy the correct quantities of raw materials (and other resources) at the correct time and from the most suitable and reliable supplier. Raw materials must be in place or production simply will not happen. This could result in a loss of customers and so a reduction in profits.

The quantity of stock to be ordered depends on the:

- current stock of raw materials available to the business
- amount of finance (money) available to purchase raw materials
- storage space available to store raw materials, for example, the size of the warehouse
- delivery/lead time – time between placing the order and the goods being delivered to the warehouse
- daily usage – the amount of raw materials used each day in the production process
- potential demand from customers for the businesses products.

SELECTING A SUPPLIER OF RAW MATERIALS

When choosing a supplier of raw materials, the operations department needs to take the following factors into account.

Quality
Is the quality of the raw materials on offer of a satisfactory standard?

Quantity
Any potential supplier of raw materials must be able to meet the quantities required by the operations department.

Dependability
Potential suppliers must be dependable, respectable, likely to stay in business and have reliable delivery systems in place.

Time
Potential suppliers of raw materials should be able to deliver by the date requested.

Price
The lowest price for the quality desired should be sought to ensure value for money. Discounts should be requested for good custom and bulk buying.

Location
If the supplier is not close by, there could be expensive delivery charges.

THE IMPORTANCE OF STAFF TRAINING

Ensuring that all employees are well trained to do the job they are employed to do is **essential** if the business wishes to produce a high quality product or service. Staff should regularly undertake a skills scan or SWOT analysis (**s**trengths, **w**eaknesses, **o**pportunities and **t**hreats) to ensure that future training and development needs are met.

The benefits of training staff include the following:
- It ensures new employees gain the necessary skills, knowledge, qualities and qualifications for the job they will be doing.
- It makes it easier for new employees to reach the level of performance expected of them by the business.
- It reduces long-term costs by minimising waste and increasing the productivity/output of each worker.
- It helps to improve the image and reputation of the business because customers will have more confidence in well-trained employees who are capable and reliable.

Disadvantages associated with training staff include the following:
- It can be very costly to put staff through training courses.
- Output and production can be lost while members of staff are being trained.

RECYCLING

Recycling is taking used materials such as glass, paper, metal, plastic, textiles and electronics and processing them into new products. Recycling makes business sense as well as environmental sense – businesses who carefully and successfully manage their resources benefit from the following:

Increased profits
Recycling helps the business to cut the costs associated with waste disposal, and being efficient with resources can save gas and electricity costs, labour costs and transportation costs.

In Scotland, businesses have to apply for a special license to deal with waste disposal. This license costs money and recycling is therefore a more attractive option.

Competitive advantage
More and more customers are seeking assurance that their suppliers are environmentally friendly. In addition, an increasing number of customers also expect that the product they buy will be made in a sustainable way, with recyclable packaging. This is now a key aspect of a quality product.

Compliance
Scotland's Zero Waste Plan sets out the Scottish Government's vision for a **zero waste society,** where:
- all waste is seen as a resource
- waste is minimised
- valuable resources are used efficiently and replaced where possible
- waste is sorted, leaving only limited amounts to be landfilled.

A business that is resource efficient and recycles will be better equipped to adapt to the forthcoming changes to legislation (law).

CASE STUDY

Head to p91 for case study 12 on Box-It.

ONLINE

PROGRESS CHECK 23: Visit www.brightredbooks.net/ N5BusMgmt and test your knowledge of quality.

ONLINE TEST

How well have you learned this topic? Take the 'Quality' test at www.brightredbooks. net/N5BusMgmt

WHAT IS PACKAGING?

Packaging is anything that is used to contain and protect raw materials or products, and is thrown away after the product is consumed (opened).

Businesses sometimes use packaging to attract customers, but this can mean an overuse of resources. There are now strict environmental regulations to minimise packaging design and make sure that most of it can be recovered or recycled.

Packaging must:
- be kept to a minimum, with only the minimum weight and volume needed to keep the product safe and hygienic
- not contain high levels of noxious or hazardous substances
- be designed so that the materials used are recyclable
- contain at least 50 per cent organic materials that burn naturally – for example, paper, wood or cardboard – if it is designed to be burnt
- be biodegradable – if it's designed for composting
- actually be reusable – if it's designed to be reusable.

 THINGS TO DO AND THINK ABOUT

Marks and Spencer have an excellent reputation for providing high quality products. This is partly achieved by ensuring new trainee managers undergo rigorous training and development.

Visit this website: http://corporate.marksandspencer.com/mscareers/opportunities/ graduates/training_and_induction

Produce a brief summary (on a sheet of A4 paper) of the types of training offered to new trainee managers at Marks and Spencer.

Explain why this contributes to the high quality products and services offered by the store.

CASE STUDIES

CASE STUDIES 1 AND 2

The following case studies provide you with the opportunity to apply your knowledge and understanding of Business Management to a range of business scenarios.

CASE STUDY 1: THE HOT PLATE

Read the case study on The Hot Plate and answer the questions that follow on A4 paper.

The Hot Plate is a small restaurant in Glasgow. It serves up traditional Scottish fare but prides itself in keeping up to date with modern cuisine. Head chef and owner Hamish McDonald has recently started a new, but flourishing, cookery school based within the premises, where customers can learn about local produce and how best to cook it. The cookery school is open on two week-day evenings.

As the owner, Hamish is responsible for the day-to-day running of the restaurant. He employs one other chef, and five other employees who each have an interest in food. They either work in the kitchen or as waiting staff. Hamish's sister Mhairi is employed to order supplies. She also pays staff wages, as well as looking after all the bookings and greeting customers on their arrival.

The Hot Plate is flourishing and has built up an excellent reputation. Hamish puts this down not only to the delicious food but also to the excellent customer service provided by his staff.

Customers often visit the restaurant or cookery school after being given a recommendation by friends or family. They are invited to tasting evenings where they can try samples of all the products available and there is a comfortable bar area where customers can sit before and after their meal.

The restaurant staff have been trained to ensure that customers' needs are the top priority, and will often go out of their way to make sure that customers have the best possible experience within the restaurant. They are trained to chat with customers in a friendly and unobtrusive way.

Hamish also trains his staff up on the ingredients used in his dishes, and encourages them to test the items on the menu, so that they can give their customers helpful, knowledgeable information in order to help them make the best decisions on their menu choices.

Questions

1   Describe all the ways that The Hot Plate has promoted excellent customer service within its restaurant. **(4 marks)**

2   Outline two positive effects of The Hot Plate having excellent customer service. **(2 marks)**

3   Describe two negative effects that would result if The Hot Plate developed a reputation for poor customer service. **(2 marks)**

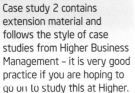

EXTENSION

Case study 2 contains extension material and follows the style of case studies from Higher Business Management – it is very good practice if you are hoping to go on to study this at Higher.

CASE STUDY 2: DELIVERING FAST FOOD FRANCHISING

Read the case study on franchising of the pizza delivery business, and then answer the questions that follow on A4 paper.

Domino's Pizza leads the UK market for home delivered pizza and is also the world's largest franchise for this type of distribution.   Para 1

Franchising means selling the rights to use a firm's logos, operating methods and brand name. Other franchised operations include Pizza Hut Express, Perfect Pizza and its partner brand Papa John's. There is also a flow of newcomers such as EasyPizza and Telepizza. In a market dominated by franchise operations, why is this type of business organisation so successful for numerous pizza brands? And why is franchising the business organisation of choice for many individuals wanting to start their own business?   Para 2

contd

Franchising or direct control?

Para 3 PizzaExpress restaurants expanded entirely through franchises during the 1970s and 1980s but the owner Gondola plc bought back the contracts in the mid 1990s. Its objective was to give the company greater control over its brand, outlets and reputation. This has been achieved, but the growth in the business has been almost half of that of franchised operations.

Para 4 Investment has not been a problem for the Pizza Hut restaurant chain in the UK, with the massive resources of Whitbread funding its growth. However, the company has decided to use the power of franchising to develop its home delivery brand, Pizza Hut Delivery, as it has identified more growth in this segment. In fact, expansion across the country has been achieved almost entirely through franchising. It is believed that there are as many as 2000 franchisees awaiting approval to own a Domino's delivery outlet alone.

Para 5 Despite losing some control over the business, franchising is a cost-effective way for an organisation to grow. Most of the set-up costs are paid by the franchisee. Additionally, the annual franchise fees go straight to the franchising company's profits. In the case of Domino's, this helped to boost their profits by 35 per cent in 2006 to £8.8 million.

Para 6 Domino's believes it can achieve a market penetration of over 1000 franchised units in Britain. An individual Domino's outlet can serve up to 20000 homes and, as the UK has around 25 million households, its projected growth and profits could continue for some time to come. The company intends to open 250 new outlets over the next five years. Similarly, Perfect Pizza plans to create more than 2000 jobs in 100 new franchised takeaways and increase its market share to 15 per cent. The company, which already has 200 outlets, intends to carry out the expansion over the next five years in the north of England and Scotland.

Advantages of franchising

Para 7 Despite the costs of buying a franchise and territory, business start-ups based on franchising have a far lower failure rate than independent firms. An entrepreneur needs cash of at least £50000 to start with well-known franchises such as Domino's and Pizza Hut. The associated risks of such a level of investment – and the need to take out additional loans – are reduced because trading strategies and methods have been tried and tested by these established brands.

Para 8 Many young people (consumers) will not use unknown independent outlets. Brands such as Pizza Hut and Dominos have wide customer loyalty, ensuring the franchised outlet has immediate demand. Additionally, large franchise businesses have marketing budgets way beyond other independent sole traders. As an example, Domino's has bought the right to use The Simpsons in its latest promotional campaign; such an investment would be impossible for a small-scale independent sole trader.

Para 9 Television advertising has played a major part in the success of Pizza Hut. To achieve good national exposure requires an investment of at least £500000; small independent (sole trader) pizza delivery services could never compete at this level.

Para 10 The potential danger for new franchises is the saturation of the pizza delivery market, over-supplied by competing brands. There are also concerns that the increasing worries about high levels of fat in our diet may eventually affect pizza sales.

Questions

Question		Para	Marks
1	State who leads the market on pizza delivery.	(1)	1
2	Explain what is meant by franchising.	(2)	2
3	State what other home pizza delivery businesses now operate as a franchise.	(2)	5
4	Explain why Pizza Express bought back all franchised outlets.	(3)	1
5	State how many franchisees are waiting to join Dominos.	(4)	1
6	Explain why franchising is considered a cost-effective way to grow.	(5)	2
7	Perfect Pizza plans to open 100 new franchises – how many new jobs will this create?	(6)	1
8	Outline why the risks of failure are lower for a franchise rather than an independent sole trader.	(7)	2
9	State what reason is given in paragraph 9 to suggest that independent sole traders are not able to compete with franchises.	(9)	1
10	Briefly outline two factors that could pose a threat to pizza franchises.	(10)	2

CASE STUDIES 3, 4 AND 5

CASE STUDY 3: RATCLIFFE FOOD

Read the case study on Ratcliffe Food and then answer the questions that follow on A4 paper.

The most recognisable Ratcliffe product is Bake-Em-Chips. Ratcliffe is Scotland's biggest producer of oven chips and buys 4 per cent of all Scottish potatoes. It is also one of Scotland's biggest frozen foods companies.

Owned privately, the company is fully focused on its market. This means that Ratcliffe often undertakes market research to find out what customers want. The products it creates are, therefore, ones which consumers want to buy.

Ratcliffe Food have diversified and also create other products than chips – including potato croquettes, crisps, roast potatoes, hash browns, potato wedges, tatty scones and waffles – which are distributed through various UK retailers such as restaurants, supermarkets etc.

As well as this, they make a range of potato shapes like Dino Potatoes, Crunchy Tots and Spell-a-tatty (shaped as letters), which younger consumers like.

Additionally, Ratcliffe produce pizzas.

Since the potato was introduced to the UK by Walter Raleigh in the 17th century, the potato chip has certainly evolved. Fish and chips were beginning to be bought in London's streets and alleyways and in some of Britain's industrial towns by the 1850s. Nowadays, fish and chips are a traditional national favourite dish!

Chips come in many different shapes and sizes, varying from the deep-fried kind served by fish and chip vendors to Ratcliffe's 8-per-cent–fat Bake-Em-Chips for home cooking.

17th century	Potato introduced by Walter Raleigh
1850	Fish and chip shops in London and major cities
1980s	Development of the oven chip
2005	Development of new varieties of low-fat and low-salt content oven chips

External challenges

In 2005/6 Ratcliffe's business was affected by a big environmental factor, the growing concern about obesity, particularly in children. This case study shows how Ratcliffe rose to this and other external challenges by developing a low-fat product.

Ratcliffe's view is that its chips can, and do, play a role in a healthy balanced diet. It is continually finding ways to ensure that its products are as healthy as possible.

Questions

1   Outline what is meant by a privately owned company.   **(1 mark)**

2   State what is meant by market research. Briefly outline one method by which
    a company can carry out market research.   **(2 marks)**

3   Briefly outline the changing factor in Ratcliffe's external social environment
    that is shaping the business's future.   **(1 mark)**

CASE STUDY 4: SCOTT'S PICS

Read the case study on Scott's Pics and then answer the questions that follow on A4 paper.

Scott's Pics has been a leader in the photographic business for decades. The Scott's Pics story began in 1980, when Bruce Scott opened a photography store as a sole trader.

Today, the company is one of the premier photographic retailer in the country, operating from over 175 stores around the UK. In addition, it has an online shop and call centre.

The modern photographic industry has changed radically. The business originally focused on producing prints from photographic film. Every shot of a reel of film was printed regardless of quality. Today, however, digital cameras allow consumers to choose which prints are produced.

As a result, traditional film printing in the UK is declining by around 30 per cent year on year. This is posing a challenge to the directors and managers at Scott's Pics. They must develop ideas and strategies to address the changing market and stimulate new demand so that they can sustain and grow the business.

Questions

1 Explain what is meant by a sole trader. Outline two advantages and two
disadvantages of operating this type of business. **(5 marks)**

2 Outline the changing factor in Scott's Pics' external technological environment that
is shaping the business's future. **(1 mark)**

CASE STUDY 5: BAD WEATHER AFFECTS CHRISTMAS DELIVERIES

Read the case study on the effect of bad weather on Christmas deliveries and then
answer the questions that follow on A4 paper.

Some internet retailers have spent millions and have had to bend over backwards to ensure that deliveries of goods arrive before Christmas this year because the bad weather and snowed under courier networks have affected Christmas deliveries.

Companies such as Marks and Spencer and John Lewis decided to bring online Christmas orders to a halt earlier than scheduled to make certain they could fulfil their deliveries on time.

Savvy shoppers have opted to order online from in front of the fire, instead of facing the heavy snow outdoors, in advance of Christmas. The rising number of people shopping online forced some listed retailers to advise the market of falling sales. However, deliveries by stretched courier services are struggling to reach parts of rural England and northern Scotland and Wales.

Dino Rocos, John Lewis's operations director spoke out about their decision to stop taking Christmas orders three days ahead of the planned cut off date. He said 'this is a hugely busy time for online sales. It's not something you do lightly'.

One of the couriers John Lewis uses to deliver online orders, Home Delivery Network, experienced unexpectedly extreme delays due to the snow. 'We had to turn to other contractors to help deliver our 1.2 million Christmas packages,' said Mr Rocos.

'[The snow] knocked us out for a couple of days, and the recovery is slow,' he said. 'As you're trying to recover from the first batch, you're hit again.'

City Link stopped processing new packages for shipment to Scotland on 16 December, and on Thursday they cautioned customers that they should anticipate delays of up to five days on deliveries to areas including Ashford and Scunthorpe in eastern England.

Questions

1 Name two well-known companies stopped taking online orders earlier
than planned. **(2 marks)**

2 Outline the main factor in the external environment that affected sales,
online orders and deliveries for the businesses mentioned in the passage. **(1 mark)**

CASE STUDIES 6, 7 AND 8

CASE STUDY 6: THOMSON HOLIDAYS

Read the case study on Thomson Holidays and then answer the questions that follow on A4 paper.

> Thomson Holidays call centre was set up at Cardonald Business Park in 1999 with help from Scottish Enterprise. It received a government grant – Regional Selective Assistance – worth £1.4 million when it opened.
>
> In December 2006 Thomson Holidays closed its Glasgow call centre with the loss of 450 jobs. More people are now choosing to book online rather than by phone. Since the centre opened in 1999, the company's internet bookings had increased from 10 per cent to 50 per cent.

Questions

1 Thomson Holidays provides a service. True or false? **(1 mark)**

2 State the sector of industry in which Thomson Holidays operates. **(1 mark)**

3 Name and describe the other two sectors of industry. **(4 marks)**

4 Identify two stakeholders who will have been affected by the closure of the call centre and describe their interest in the business. **(4 marks)**

5 Explain how the interests of employees might conflict with those of the management of Thomson Holidays, who are primarily concerned with increasing sales and profits. **(2 marks)**

CASE STUDY 7: HOWSTERS

Read the case study on Howsters and then answer the questions that follow on A4 paper.

> Howsters is a high street retail store which uses a variety of methods to engage with its different stakeholder groups. For example, the company uses initiatives such as the community engagement programme in India to communicate with workers and their communities in the countries that manufacture its goods. Howsters understands that different stakeholder groups have different needs and expectations. As such, it uses appropriate channels of communication to engage with each stakeholder group.

Questions

1 State the sector of industry that Howsters operates in. **(1 mark)**

2 State the sector of the economy in which Howsters operates. **(1 mark)**

3 Identify as many stakeholders in Howsters as you can. **(6 marks)**

4 Explain why Howsters is trying to work with all stakeholders. **(2 marks)**

CASE STUDY 8: ASDA – MEETING STAKEHOLDER NEEDS THROUGH COMMUNITY INVOLVEMENT

Read the case study on Asda and then answer the questions that follow on A4 paper.

Introduction

Asda is the second largest UK retailer, with over 600 stores in the UK and 180 000 employees. Customer loyalty is extremely important, especially in a highly competitive market such as supermarket retailing. Competing on price helps to retain customers, but so does non-price competition such as having a good image in the community.

Mission statements

Asda makes clear statements about its mission, purpose and values to help stakeholders see the direction the business is taking. New employees receive a detailed induction.

Stakeholders

Asda has both internal stakeholders (within the business) and external stakeholders. Examples of internal stakeholders are managers and employees. Examples of external stakeholders are customers and shareholders. Stakeholders can want different things:

- Customers want low-priced, good quality products. They also want to see that Asda is involved positively in their community.
- Employees are motivated by a good career structure and by being able to help the community.
- Shareholders want a good return on their investment but they also believe in community involvement, as it makes good business sense.
- Suppliers may be local businesses that Asda can use.

Community programme

The Community Life programme has been running since 2012. The initiative's aim is to get all Asda's UK stores playing an even more central role in their local community.

Each store has a Community Life Champion who works one day a week with community groups and local organisations. They also arrange events in store and inspire colleagues and customers to get involved in local community work.

Benefits for stakeholders

Different stakeholder groups benefit in different ways. Customers gain from the improvement in their local and wider community. Employees gain by helping to make these improvements and by feeling more valued. Working with the community has become a source of staff motivation.

Conclusion

Organisations in competitive markets need to keep customer loyalty. Asda's method involves gaining loyalty by having a positive effect on the communities in which it works.

Questions

1 Define what is meant by the term 'stakeholder'. **(1 mark)**

2 Copy and complete the following diagram.

(4 marks)

3 Explain the difference between internal and external stakeholders. **(2 marks)**

4 List two examples of internal stakeholders and two examples of external stakeholders. **(4 marks)**

5 For each of the following stakeholders, state their aim and how they can influence Asda:

- customers
- employees
- government
- local community.

(8 marks)

CASE STUDIES 9, 10, 11 AND 12

CASE STUDY 9: GREEN'S

Green's is a well-known DIY store. Green's value their employees and have put together a package of benefits which is designed to encourage them to want to stay with the company.

Read the case study on Green's and then answer the questions that follow on A4 paper.

Employee Benefits

We reward our colleagues with a competitive rewards package:

- There are various bonus schemes to celebrate our success.
- Discount cards offering 20 per cent off Green's products, in store or online.
- Our Employee Benefit Book offers discounts on everyday products and services.
- Green's supports working parents by offering childcare vouchers allowing significant savings.

Bonus Schemes

Our bonus schemes are designed to drive performance and to reward accordingly. For this reason, they are built around a series of measures at both company and local level. A number of bonus schemes are operated at Green's, each designed to allow our employees to share in the success of our business. Our bonus schemes are reviewed annually to ensure they remain competitive within the marketplace.

The Green's Staff Card entitles employees to receive a fantastic 20 per cent discount on most purchases at any Green's store as well as online orders.

Green's recognises employees who really make a difference and celebrates outstanding contributions at an annual awards event.

Eligible employees benefit from enhanced maternity, paternity and adoption policies offering over and above the statutory requirements.

At Green's, all permanent employees, irrespective of service or caring responsibilities, have the right to request flexible working, giving an opportunity to achieve more balance between work and other commitments.

Employees can refer talented people with a passion for retail and service delivery to lead our business forward – if the individual you refer is successful, you will receive a bonus payment.

Green's employees can enjoy various discounts at high street retailers, travel, leisure and other great places.

All of our employees are entitled to 6.6 weeks' annual leave.

Our competitive pension scheme is offered through our group company. Employees are eligible to join this pension scheme.

In recognition of long service, employees are awarded additional annual leave and a bonus payment on specific anniversary dates.

Payroll giving is the simplest tax effective way for employees to give to their favourite charities.

Green's supports working parents with childcare costs through the provision of the Government Childcare Voucher Scheme – this is non-taxable and exempt from National Insurance, allowing significant savings to be made.

Green's employees are offered a corporate discount on their membership to one of the largest health plan providers in the UK.

Questions

1   Outline three reasons why you think Green's want to retain their existing workforce.
(3 marks)

2   State how Green's supports those employees who are working parents.   **(1 mark)**

3   Briefly describe how Green's celebrates the success of those workers who have worked hard and made a real contribution to the business.   **(1 mark)**

4   Outline how Green's supports those employees who want a better work-life balance.   **(1 mark)**

5   State how Green's rewards long-serving employees.   **(1 mark)**

6   State the two main factors that drive Green's bonus schemes.   **(2 marks)**

CASE STUDY 10: DOGGYCHOCS

Read the case study on DoggyChocs and answer the questions that follow on A4 paper.

Jem and Irma have come up with a great idea. They have produced a new type of dog treat called DoggyChocs, which is very popular with their own pets. Their plan is to sell DoggyChocs to outlets in their local area in packets that Irma is designing. They are not sure whether DoggyChocs will be bought by enough people or what price to charge them or even where to sell from. They want some evidence to prove that their DoggyChocs product will be a success. This means carrying out some market research!

Questions

1   Explain why you think it is important for all businesses to have information about their market.   **(1 mark)**

2   Outline two pieces of information that you think are important for Jem and Irma to find out.   **(2 marks)**

3   Outline the advice that you would give to Jem and Irma to enable them to collect the information they need.   **(1 mark)**

CASE STUDY 11: JUICEBOX

Read the case study on Juicebox and then answer the questions that follow on A4 paper.

Juicebox – a new soft drink organisation – has come up with the idea of an orange drink in a carton, with an integrated straw. Once the box has been opened, the straw pops out.

Juicebox intends its target market to be children. The company will take samples of the product out to the High Street and find out what the general public think of the idea.

Questions

1   Explain what is meant by 'primary information'.   **(1 mark)**

2   List three pieces of primary information that Juicebox should collect when conducting market research.   **(3 marks)**

ONLINE CASE STUDY 12: BOX-IT

Read the case study on Box-It and then answer the questions that follow on A4 paper.

Packaging is important: it protects our products, allows us to transport them safely, and ultimately saves far more energy than it consumes. At the same time, it can end up as waste, particularly in those countries where the infrastructure for recycling is poor. Our approach to this is to reduce, reuse and recycle.

We are reducing the weight of our packaging by using stronger, lighter-weight materials. We are also making our packaging more recyclable and aim to use more recycled material ourselves.

Our analysis has highlighted that our food packaging is one of the biggest contributors to our waste footprint. But to achieve our goal we will need to reduce waste across all product categories by reducing the weight of packaging and by helping to increase recycling. Tea bags form a significant proportion of product leftovers.

Questions

1   Outline the reasons why Box-It say packaging is important to their business. **(2 marks)**

2   State three actions Box-It are taking to address their concerns about packaging.   **(3 marks)**

3   Suggest one way that Box-It might be able to use recycled materials.   **(2 marks)**

SUGGESTED ANSWERS/SOLUTIONS FOR CASE STUDIES

All answers should be written to reflect the command word used in each question.

CASE STUDY 1: THE HOT PLATE

Possible answers/solutions

1 The Hot Plate has developed excellent customer service by greeting customers on arrival to the restaurant, offering tasting evenings for customers to try samples of their food and training all staff to ensure they know customer service is a priority. They also ensure staff taste the food and are familiar with the ingredients in order that they can give helpful information to customers.

2 Good customer service has resulted in The Hot Plate developing a good reputation and attracting more customers.

3 Two negative effects for The Hot Plate if they developed a reputation for poor customer service would be, loss of customers, increased customer complaints and a fall in profits.

CASE STUDY 2: DELIVERING FAST FOOD FRANCHISING

Possible answers/solutions

1 Domino's leads the market on pizza delivery.

2 Franchising is when a person (franchisee) starts a business and provides a product or service supplied by another business (franchisor). The franchisee is allowed to use the franchisor's business name and sell its products.

3 Other home pizza delivery services which now operate as a franchise are EasyPizza, Telepizza and Papa John's.

4 Pizza Express bought back franchised outlets because they wanted more control over its brand, outlets and reputation.

5 2000 franchisees are waiting to join Dominoes

6 Franchising is a cost-effective way to grow as it can achieve market penetration and increased market share relatively quickly.

7 Perfect Pizza will create 2000 jobs with the creation of 100 new franchises.

8 Risks are lower for a franchiser because trading strategies and methods have been tried and tested.

9 Sole traders are not able to compete with franchises because they do not have the necessary finance to achieve television exposure.

10 Two factors that could pose a threat to pizza franchises are market saturation (too many suppliers) of the market and increasing concerns about fat in consumers' diets.

CASE STUDY 3: RATCLIFFE FOOD

Possible answers/solutions

1 A privately owned company is a company who does not sell its shares on the stock market.

2 Market research is any activity which seeks to find out the wants and needs of customers. Methods of market research include surveys, consumer focus groups, hall tests and sampling.

3 The changing factor in Ratcliffe's external social factor is obesity, especially in children. Ratcliffe responded by developing low-fat chips.

CASE STUDY 4: SCOTT'S PICS

Possible answers/solutions

1 A sole trader is a business owned by one person. The advantages are that the owner can make all the decisions, and keep all the profits. The disadvantages are that the owner has unlimited liability and the sole trader can find it difficult to obtain finance.

2 Scott's Pics' external technological environment is changing because of digital cameras. Digital cameras allow consumers to choose what prints are produced and so traditional film production is declining.

CASE STUDY 5: BAD WEATHER AFFECTS CHRISTMAS DELIVERIES

Possible answers/solutions

1 John Lewis and Marks and Spencer stopped taking online orders earlier than was planned.

2 The external environmental factor that affected sales, online orders and deliveries was the weather (snow).

CASE STUDY 6: THOMSON HOLIDAYS

Possible answers/solutions

1 True.
2 Thomson Holidays operates in the tertiary sector.
3 The two other sectors of industry are primary and secondary. Businesses in the primary sector extract resources from the Earth such as farming, coal mining and fishing. Businesses in the secondary sector are involved in manufacturing, for example, cars and televisions.
4 Two stakeholders who would have been affected by the closure of Thomson Holiday's call centre are employees and Management. Employees would have been concerned about being made unemployed and Management would have been concerned about loss of status, bonus and possible position within the organisation.
5 Employees are concerned about fair pay and job security. Management are concerned about reducing costs to increase profits. Conflict could occur if management tried to reduce staffing levels in an attempt to reduce business costs.

CASE STUDY 7: HOWSTERS

Possible answers/solutions

1 Howsters operates in the tertiary sector – they provide a retail service.
2 Howsters operates in the private sector of the economy.
3 Stakeholders in Howsters are suppliers, board of directors or management, customers, government, employees, banks and other lenders, shareholders etc.
4 Howsters is trying to work with all stakeholders because all stakeholders have a vested interest in the business and many have power to influence the business. For example, workers can strike, suppliers can change credit terms and customers can take their business elsewhere.

CASE STUDY 8: ASDA – MEETING STAKEHOLDER NEEDS THROUGH COMMUNITY INVOLVEMENT

Possible answers/solutions

1 A stakeholder is any person or any business who is interested in an organisation's success.
2 Stakeholders in Asda would include customers, employees, suppliers, government, shareholders and management.
3 Internal stakeholders are within the organisation and external stakeholders are outwith the organisation.
4 Examples of internal stakeholders are management and employees. Examples of external stakeholders are government and suppliers.
5 Customers can take their business to a competitor of Asda, eg, Tesco. Employees could strike if they feel their working conditions are unfair. Government could increase corporation tax on Asda's profits. The local community could complain about pollution or noise caused by a large supermarket in their community.

CASE STUDY 9: GREEN'S

Possible answers/solutions

1 Three reasons why Green's want to retain their existing workforce are that they have spent money training staff and would then have to spend more money training new staff; recruiting new staff is costly and time-consuming; and when staff are continually leaving there can be a loss of team spirit in an organisation.
2 Green's supports working parents through the provision of the Government Childcare Voucher Scheme.
3 Green's celebrates the success of those employees who have worked hard and made a real contribution to the business at their annual awards event.
4 Green's supports those workers who want a better work-life balance by offering flexible working patterns.
5 Green's rewards long serving employees by offering additional annual leave and bonus payments on specific anniversary dates.
6 The two factors that drive Green's's bonus schemes are people with talent and a passion for retail and service delivery.

CASE STUDY 10: DOGGYCHOCS

Possible answers/solutions

1 It is important for all businesses to have information about the market in which they operate to ensure they are meeting the needs and wants of consumers.
2 They should try to find out what price consumers are willing to pay (Price) for their product and the best Place to sell their product. They could also look at what would be the best way to promote their product to the market.
3 They should carry out market research.

CASE STUDY 11: JUICEBOX

Possible answers/solutions

1 Primary information is new information that has been gathered by an organisation and will be used for a specific purpose.
2 Three pieces of primary information that Juicebox should collect when conducting market research are – how much consumers will be willing to pay; consumer feedback having sampled the product/drink, would consumers purchase the drink from Juicebox instead of the drinks they normally purchase; and what market segment/s will purchase the product etc.

CASE STUDY 12: BOX-IT

Possible answers/solutions

1 Packaging is important because it protects the product and allows products to be transported safely.
2 Reduce, reuse and recycle.
3 They could use recycled paper for labels and packaging.

GLOSSARY

appraisal
a report on how well an employee is progressing. It's usually carried out once a year

apprenticeship
usually involves on-the-job and off-the-job training, where the apprentice works and trains in the workplace for part of the week, and attends college for the rest of the week

aptitude tests
measure how good the applicant is at a particular skill, for example, mathematical skills, keyboard skills, shorthand speeds or driving ability

batch production
the production of groups of similar products. No item in a group goes on to the next stage until all are ready

benchmarking
identifying a benchmark – that is, identifying another organisation commonly regarded as the 'best' in the industry and copying their best techniques – is sometimes used as a method of improving the quality of production of a good or service

brand
a name, symbol, design (or a combination of all these) that the producer uses to make the product instantly recognisable

break-even point
the level of production where total costs = total revenue – that is, when no profit or loss is made

business cycle
the process involved in buying and selling goods and services

capital intensive production
a production system that achieves high output levels because it is automated. This means that machines do the work instead of people

cash budget
a plan of how much money you have and how you will spend it

central government
comprises Westminster Parliament (Houses of Parliament) and the Scottish Parliament

charities
set up to help a charitable cause, and generally exempt from paying most taxes

coaching
a trainer takes a trainee through a task, step-by-step. The trainer is always on hand to support and coach the trainee. The idea is that the 'coach' will pass on their skills and knowledge to the trainee by being a mentor

curriculum vitae
means 'life history'. CVs are prepared by most job applicants and provide a short summary of their career achievements to date

customer service
provision of service to a customer before, during and after a purchase

desk research
researchers use secondary information in the form of published sources – for example, the internet; government department reports; market research reports published by companies such as Keynote; competitors' websites; voters' roles and trade magazines

differentiated marketing
involves targeting each market segment with a product or service specifically designed to match the needs of those consumers within the segment.

durable
long lasting

employment legislation
three key pieces of employment legislation are:
> Health and Safety at Work Act 1974
> Data Protection Act 1998
> Freedom of Information (Scotland) Act 2002

entrepreneur
an individual who creates and develops a business idea to produce a product or service that makes a profit

external factors
PESTEC: the six key external factors that affect a business: **p**olitical; **e**conomic; **s**ocial; **t**echnological; **e**nvironmental and **c**ompetitive

external recruitment
looks for suitable candidates outside the organisation

factors of production
land, labour, capital and enterprise

field research
researchers go out 'into the field' to obtain first-hand, primary information for the organisation to use

flow production
a process in which the production of items moves continuously from one operation to the next. Each part of the process contributes to the eventual production of the final product. Usually, machinery or robots are employed to reduce labour costs. Products are produced to a standard specification

franchise
a business agreement where one business can operate under the name of another business

gap in the market
an idea for a product or service that is not currently being offered

Human Resource Management (HRM)
refers to the function within an organisation that recruits, trains, develops and maintains an effective workforce

'in-basket' tasks
candidates are asked to look through a manager's 'in-basket' of letters, memos, mail, and reports. These contain a number of problems that have to be addressed. Candidates are then asked to examine them, prioritise them and respond appropriately with problem-solving strategies

internal factors
the five key internal factors that affect a business: finance; staff; management; information and technology

internal recruitment
looks for suitable candidates from staff who already work for the organisation

job analysis
a way of identifying whether a job can be shared, or whether there is no need to fill a vacancy

job production
where a single product is custom made to a customer's own specification

job rotation
a trainee learns tasks in different departments/jobs. This is how supermarkets usually train employees, by rotating them round different departments such as checkout, clothing, home products, bakery and electrics.

job specification/description
lists all of the duties that will be involved in the job

Just in Time (JIT) production
a Japanese approach that keeps the stock levels (and therefore costs) to a minimum. Stock is ordered and arrives just in time to be used in production. Goods are not produced unless the firm has an order from a customer

knowledge tests
involve specific questions to determine how much the individual knows about particular job tasks and responsibilities

labour intensive production
a production system that uses humans rather than machinery to produce goods – particularly where a single product or a few of the same types of product are being produced – for example, designer dresses

leaderless tasks
a group of candidates is asked to respond to various problems and challenges, without a designated group leader. Candidates are evaluated on their behaviour in the group discussions. This could include their teamwork skills, their interaction with others or their leadership skills.

local government (councils)
these are set up by central government to run day-to-day services at a local level

market
a place where **buyers** and **sellers** come together. A market does not have to be a physical place – for example, a lot of buying and selling now takes place on the internet

market orientation
an organisation with a market-orientated approach (or a market-led organisation) thinks that its most important asset is its customers

market research
involves the constant gathering, recording and analysing of data about an organisation's product/services and its target market of customers to grow and survive

market research
a way of measuring customer satisfaction

market segmentation
involves splitting consumers into different groups or segments and then marketing a product/service directly to those groups

marketing concept
the idea that a business organisation has to identify and meet the demands, needs and wants of customers to grow and survive

marketing mix
this consists of what is known as the 'four Ps': product, price, promotion and place

non-durable
used up quickly

off-the-job training
this involves employees attending courses away from their workplace, for example, at colleges or universities

operations
the name given to the process of turning raw materials into finished articles – products ready to be offered for sale to consumers

partnership
a business with two to 20 partners

person specification
outlines the skills, qualifications, experience and qualities that the ideal candidate should possess

personality tests
aim to determine whether the applicant is a team player or not, and what team role or roles they perform best – for example, are they a team leader, or do they contribute specialist skills to a team?

Physical ability tests
often used by the police, fire brigade and army to test strength, endurance and physical speed and coordination.

place
where the customer can buy the product or service – how accessible it is

price
the amount that the customer has to pay for the product/service

primary sector
businesses in this sector use natural resources

private limited company (Ltd)
has shares that are owned privately

private sector
this sector consists of the following types of business organisation: sole trader; partnership; private limited company (Ltd); public limited company (plc) and franchise

product
the good/service that is being sold

product life cycle
the four stages of the product lifecycle are introduction, growth, maturity and decline

product orientation
an organisation with a product-orientated (or asset-led) approach to marketing and selling tries to sell whatever it can make without trying to find out if it's what the consumers want. It simply looks at the assets and strengths of the business to determine what products it should make and sell. Apple is an example of this.

profit and loss account
prepared after the gross profit is calculated in the trading account. All the current year's expenses are deducted from the gross profit, resulting in the **net profit**

promotion
how the customer is made aware of the product/service

psychometric tests
are designed to measure the intellectual ability, personality, attitudes and character of the applicant. These are usually timed, multiple-choice tests, taken under exam conditions.

public corporation
companies that are owned and controlled by central government

public limited company (plc)
has shares available for purchase by the public on the stock market

public sector
this sector consists of the following types of business organisation: central government; local government and public corporation

purchasing mix
the factors that need to be considered when deciding on a supplier: raw materials; price; quality; quantity; reliability; delivery; credit; location

Quality assurance procedures
At certain points in the production process, products are checked to ensure that they meet agreed quality standards. All aspects of the production process are looked at to ensure errors do not occur. There is more emphasis on workers self-checking rather than checking by inspectors

Quality circles
These involve small groups of workers meeting at regular intervals to discuss where improvements can be made in the production process

Quality control procedures
a manufacturer passes a sample of raw materials and/or the final product through a quality control check. Any unacceptable products are then discarded as waste, or sent back for reworking

reference checks
verify that the information provided by the candidate about their education, employment history and achievements is correct

role-play exercises
candidates are asked to pretend that they already have the job and must interact with another employee to solve a given problem. The other employee is usually a trained assessor.

secondary sector
businesses in this sector make or manufacture products

sectors of industry
there are three sectors of industry: **primary**, **secondary** and **tertiary**

sectors of the economy
there are three sectors of the economy: the **private sector**, the **public sector** and the **third, or voluntary, sector**

self-paced/distance learning
employee is given resources such as a training manual and works on their own, usually at home

'sitting next to Nellie'
involves an experienced employee demonstrating a task to a trainee, who then undertakes the task. The experienced employee supports the trainee until they are totally competent at the task.

skill scan
a document that is completed by the employee and the employer. It allows both parties to consider the strengths and any weaknesses in the employee's performance, and to compare each other's views of the work being done

social enterprise
a business that has a social and/or environmental purpose

sole trader
one-owner business

stakeholders
a person or group of people who have an interest in a business or organisation, and in the way it is managed and run

structured interview
has characteristics such as standardised questions, trained interviewers, specific question order, controlled length of time and a standardised response evaluation format

Survival and growth
during a recession businesses seek to survive. In economic good times they may try and grow larger. Survival and/or growth is a feature/aim of all organisations

tertiary sector
businesses in this sector offer services, not products

third/voluntary sector
this sector consists of the following types of business organisation: charities; social clubs and voluntary organisations and social enterprises

Total Quality Management (TQM)
this is the most complete form of quality control. It tries to create a 'quality culture', encouraging everybody – from the Managing Director to the cleaners – to think about quality in everything they do. Every employee sets out to satisfy the customer. Customers are placed at the centre of the production process. Providing customers with the best quality product/service is the focus of every stage in the process, from the initial order to dispatch of the final good

trading account
shows the profit or loss made from purchasing goods at one price (the cost price) and selling them at a higher price (the selling price). The aim of the Trading Account is to calculate **gross profit**

unstructured interview
usually done 'off the cuff' with untrained interviewers, random questions and no consideration of time

voluntary organisations
run and staffed by volunteers

work-sample or performance tests
require the individual to demonstrate or perform one or more job tasks

work shadowing
involves a new member of staff following an experienced member of staff for a specified period of time so they can observe them at work and understand how they do their job